BIOLOGY and CRIME

David C. Rowe
University of Arizona

Foreword by

David P. Farrington
Cambridge University

Roxbury Publishing Company
Los Angeles, California

Library of Congress Cataloging-in-Publication Data

Rowe, David C.
Biology and crime / David C. Rowe.
p. cm.
Foreword by David Farrington. Includes bibliographical references and index.
ISBN 1-891487-80-9
1. Criminal anthropology. 2. Criminal behavior. I. Title.
HV6115.R595 2002
364.2'4–dc21 2001019793
CIP

BIOLOGY AND CRIME

Publisher: Claude Teweles
Managing Editor: Dawn VanDercreek
Production Editor: Jim Ballinger
Copyeditor: Jackie Estrada
Proofreaders: David Marion, Roger Mensink
Production Assistant: Renée Burkhammer
Indexing: Kate Sterner
Typography: Synergistic Data Systems
Cover Design: Marnie Kenney

Printed on acid-free paper in the United States of America. This book meets the standards for recycling of the Environmental Protection Agency.

ISBN 1-891487-80-9

Roxbury Publishing Company
P.O. Box 491044
Los Angeles, California 90049-9044
Voice: (310) 473-3312 • Fax: (310) 473-4490
E-mail: roxbury@roxbury.net
Website: www.roxbury.net

The Roxbury Series in Crime, Justice, and Law

Series Coeditors:

Ronald L. Akers, University of Florida

Gary F. Jensen, Vanderbilt University

This new series features concisely and cogently written books on an array of important topics, including specific types of crime and central or emerging issues in criminology, justice, and law.

The books in this series are designed and written specifically for classroom use in criminology, sociology, deviance, delinquency, criminal justice, and related classes. The intent of the series is to provide both an introduction to the issues and the latest knowledge available—at a level accessible to undergraduate students. ✦

Contents

Foreword

At one time, the influence of biological factors on crime was a taboo subject for criminologists, at least for those trained in sociology (see Sagarin 1980, 8–9). The leading textbook of criminology up to the 1970s, by Sutherland and Cressey (1974), clearly rejected the importance of biological factors. Implicitly or explicitly, it was assumed that crime was caused by nonbiological factors: society, culture, subcultures, families, schools, peers, and so on. Happily, things have now changed. Leading criminologists now believe that a comprehensive theory of crime must include biological factors as well as "the usual suspects."

In the last 20 years, there has been an enormous increase in research on biology and crime. The author of this book, David Rowe, is one of the most brilliant and gifted researchers in this field. In his book *The Limits of Family Influence* (1994), he argued—provocatively but persuasively—that any study of the influence of family factors on crime should be designed to take into account the importance of genetic factors. More generally, it can be contended that any study of the influence of environmental factors on crime (e.g., socioeconomic status, communities, peer groups, and so on) should be designed to include the importance of biological factors and to investigate interactions between biological and environmental factors (see Raine, Brennan, Farrington, and Mednick 1997).

Unfortunately, few criminologists have anything approaching an adequate training in biology. Furthermore, there are few readable expositions of research on biology and crime, although one noteworthy exception is the excellent book by Adrian Raine (1993). I am delighted to welcome David Rowe's book as a concise but superb, well-researched, and up-to-date presentation of research in this field. Hopefully, it should succeed in educating present and future generations of criminologists, and it should be of great interest to students and scholars in such other disciplines as psychology, psychiatry, sociology, and social work. This book is clearly written and spiced up with anecdotes and case histories in an entertaining fashion.

David Rowe's basic thesis is that crime, like all behavior, has a biological basis. In chapter 2, he explains the concepts of heritability and phenotypes versus genotypes, reviewing twin, adoption, and sibling studies. In chapter 3, he examines the evolutionary perspective and focuses on sexual competition for mates and sex differences in offending. Read this chapter and find out about "cad" males versus "dad" males! Chapter 4 contains an excellent review of important biological topics such as testosterone, serotonin, heart rate, and skin conductance, as well as a discussion of results obtained with modern brain-imaging techniques. In explaining psychophysiological results, Dr. Rowe prefers low arousal to fearlessness as the key factor.

In contrast to the review of behavior genetics in chapter 2, molecular genetics is described in chapter 5. Molecular genetics is an exciting and rapidly developing field. Although (of course) no single gene causes a person to be criminal, single genes have been discovered that are related to attention deficit hyperactivity disorder and novelty-seeking behavior. Chapter 6 reviews environmental influences (especially from peers and siblings) in the light of genetic findings, as well as genotype x environment interactions. Dr. Rowe concludes that evidence of genetic influences on crime should not discourage experimental tests of crime-reduction methods based on policy changes and targeted social interventions. Chapter 7 concludes the book by describing some ethical and legal issues arising from biological research on crime, such as the value of medication compared with criminal justice treatment and the use of genetic knowledge to predict offending and choose appropriate treatments for offenders.

I am delighted to recommend this book to anyone who is interested in finding out about modern knowledge on biology and crime. They will (as I did) learn a great deal about this important, exciting, and fast-developing field.

—David P. Farrington
Professor of Psychological Criminology
Cambridge University

References

Raine, A. 1993. *The Psychopathology of Crime: Criminal Behavior as a Clinical Disorder.* San Diego, CA: Academic Press.

Raine, A., P. A. Brennan, D. P. Farrington, and S. A. Mednick (Eds.) 1997. *Biosocial Bases of Violence.* New York: Plenum.

Rowe, D. C. 1994. *The Limits of Family Influence: Genes, Experience, and Behavior.* New York: Guilford.

Sagarin, E. (Ed.) 1980. *Taboos in Criminology.* Beverly Hills, CA: Sage.

Sutherland, E. H. and D. R. Cressey. 1974. *Criminology,* 9th ed. Philadelphia: Lippincott. ✦

Author's Note

A book is always a collaborative project. I particularly wish to thank Martin Daly for reviewing sections of the chapter on evolutionary views of crime and David Lykken for providing me his illustration of time trends in crime. I am grateful to other authors who contributed figures and tables to the book. Terrie Moffitt gave me insights into the association between platelet serotonin levels and crime. I must also thank a former student who, although he is not aggressive, agreed to serve as the poster-man for testosterone. At Roxbury Publishing Company, I acknowledge the encouragement by editor Claude Teweles, the management of my book's production by Jim Ballinger, and work by the copyeditor that improved the book's language. Carol Bender provided me with useful comments on the original manuscript. I have made every effort to be accurate in the book, but I take responsibility for any errors that may remain. I hope that students find the book as enjoyable to read as I found it a pleasure to write. The biology of crime is a topic of endless fascination.

The author also wants to acknowledge his debt to the many colleagues who reviewed the manuscript. Their guidance and suggestions proved to be very useful: Ronald C. Akers (*University of Florida*), Gary Jensen (*Vanderbilt University*), Alex Piquero (*Northeastern University*), Anthony Walsh (*Boise State University*), and Richard A. Wright (*Arkansas State University*). ✦

Chapter 1

Introduction to Biology and Crime

Crime is not a new problem in society. Aristotle complained about the unruliness of youth. Cities in medieval times were always dangerous, and even today European castles are well stocked with the instruments of torture used in the suppression of crime (and political opponents) during the Middle Ages. Despite a wider choice of controls in those times than those available today, crime was never eliminated.

Crime is found cross-culturally. Tribal societies recognize the danger presented by men (and less often by women) who violate the trust of social relationships; such people are ostracized or treated even more brutally. Moreover, endemic levels of murder and spousal abuse characterize some tribal societies (Chagnon 1988). Yet we pay more attention to current headlines than to the historical and cross-cultural record of human unruliness. Delinquent gangs plague inner cities. Horrible shootings have occurred in middle-class schools. In a society that has mastered spaceflight and the instant communications of the Internet, we must still lock our houses, turn on our car alarms, and avoid city parks after dark. The inability to eliminate crime speaks of a complex social failure: Why is crime so persistent and recalcitrant to our best efforts at amelioration?

One answer to this question is that crime is a part of human nature, a legacy of evolution—something deep inside the older parts of the brain, those sections sandwiched between respiration and higher thought. As pointed out in *Demonic Males* (Wrangham and

Peterson 1996), males' propensity toward violence is noticeably shared by the common chimpanzee, in which males of one troop gang up on and kill a lone male of another. In a fictionalized account of this process, the novel *Brazzaville Beach* contrasted warring humans and warring chimpanzees in an imaginary African country (Boyd 1990). Are Belgian mercenary pilots aggressive because of a biological kinship with warring chimps?

This view of crime, a biological and evolutionary view, was prominent in criminology in the nineteenth century. The criminal (typically male) was seen as atavistic because the characteristics of his evolutionary ancestors appeared in him; he was a throwback to the apes. His eyebrows extended outward on bony bumps, his jaw was large, and his skull was misshapen. His face glares out from the pages of an old book with unbridled hostility. This representation of the criminal was widely accepted for a time, but extensive measurements of the facial features of actual criminals found them to be less atavistic and far more varied than the nineteenth century science of phrenology allowed. Empirical research is always a good antidote for misconceptions, even highly popular ones. After the late nineteenth and early twentieth centuries, the theory that a criminal is born into his propensity toward crime fell into disfavor.

This book is about biology and crime. It revisits the biological basis of criminality from the perspective of the modern sciences: behavioral and molecular genetics, neural imaging, evolutionary theory, and other new approaches. The argument that a biological basis exists for criminality raises several important questions. Seeking the answers to them is a focus of this book, even though the task cannot be completed here. These questions encompass whether criminal behavior is "normal" or "abnormal," whether the physiological effects are specific to criminality or are more general, whether crime is evolutionarily adaptive or maladaptive, and so on. Merely tagging a behavior as "biological" really says little about its substance. *All behavior is biological,* unless one is a dualist and believes in a mind separate from the brain: All behavior is represented in the brain, in its biochemistry, electrical activity, structure, and growth and decline. Behavior cannot occur without biology, anymore than a computer could be run without a material central processor made of silicon, fired up by real electrons in electrical current. The central issue is whether this biology helps us to understand criminal behavior. Is the phrase a "gene for crime" in any way meaningful, and if so, how?

This book cannot be a treatise in biology. It is said that a typical biology textbook introduces as many terms as a course in a foreign language. Because many people lack a background in biology, they are unprepared to discourse on these topics. This book cannot both tackle the biology of criminality and teach biology. I have tried to use biological terms sparingly and to define them as they are introduced; I have translated other concepts into a layperson's vocabulary. Anyone interested in this topic is encouraged to learn more about genetics and evolution, because the information in this book best benefits a prepared mind.

Neither is this intended as a comprehensive textbook. It is a primer because it surveys topics superficially and does not thoroughly review the research literature. The book contains the opinions of the author. Whereas most textbooks tend to speak with an air of complete and omnipotent authority, this one was not handed down from a mountaintop; rather, it was produced on a word processor (next to stale coffee and legal pads).

A book about the biology of crime must be about the biology of criminals—about their traits, physiology, motives, and so on. Yet what is or is not criminal varies somewhat across historical periods and cultures. Some social deconstructionists might say that crime is entirely an arbitrary cultural invention and that any identification of particular people as criminals is therefore purely arbitrary. Believers in the Ten Commandments would argue for the universality of at least some criminal acts. Murder and adultery, for example, are both prohibited throughout the world; in the United States today, one is a crime that carries serious penalties and the other is made illegal in many states by rarely enforced statutes. In almost any culture, if you steal someone else's food, kill your adversaries, or lie about your commitments, you violate both laws and social norms; in tribal societies, the norms are usually not codified as written laws, but they still exist.

In short, there is enough commonality among the kinds of acts that are socially prohibited to go forward. Furthermore, a socially constructed nature of a behavior does not prevent its genetic analysis. For example, classical music instruments were invented in Europe and are now used worldwide (excellent symphony orchestras are found in Japan; a Japanese bagpipe ensemble even performed in New York's St. Patrick's Day parade). Nonetheless, a twin study could be conducted of the biological basis of musicians' performance ability on classical instruments.

We could take another not entirely satisfying approach and define crime as "that which self-report crime scales measure," much as intelligence (IQ) is sometimes called, "that which IQ tests measure." This approach is certainly not a legalistic one, because not all acts listed on such scales violate the criminal code; for example, lying to one's parents is offensive, but not necessarily criminal. In practical terms, however, we are often left with whatever method was used in any given study to measure crime.

Many of the traits we will look at are not criminal but are associated with a greater risk of committing criminal acts. Attention deficit hyperactivity disorder (ADHD), for instance, occurs in 3 to 5 percent of boys and increases the risk of criminal behavior when they grow up. Thus, by necessity, this book covers crime and criminal disposition—those characteristics associated with crime because of shared common causes. Despite these cautions, I can offer the following biologically oriented definition of crime: "Criminal acts are those acts intended to exploit people belonging to one's own social group in ways that reduce their fitness."

The smart thing to do at this point would be to leave this definition behind and move on, if only because any definition is bound to be imperfect and able to spark controversy. Nevertheless, here are my essential points. *Exploit* means to hurt or bring harm to. The acts harm others; violence clearly does so by causing death or injury, but theft takes away property and so causes an "injury" to a person's future prospects. By *fitness,* I mean the ability to survive and raise a family. Can a crime reduce the fitness of someone who intends to remain celibate? Probably not, but I prefer a definition with an evolutionary flavor because it has the broadest possible application, to humans and to nonhuman animals as well. "In ways that harm them" could be substituted for "reduce fitness" for a more *Homo sapien*-specific definition. Intention is included in the definition to eliminate accidents that harm others. A momentary distraction that leads one motorist to rear end another is not a crime like robbing a Circle K store. The degree of conscious intention behind a crime, however, is again not self-evident and is worth further consideration. Finally, my definition focuses on group membership: Crime is directed against one's fellows, people ordinarily belonging to the same tribe or country. This stipulation is made to distinguish criminal acts from warfare.

Although war is the occasion of violence and a source of much human misery, and although looting, plundering, and rape are not infrequent companions of war, this book is not about war. War is recognized by a society as legally sanctioned; warriors are given medals and honors for killing the enemy. Two evolutionarily oriented scholars have equated crime with social parasitism, because a social parasite expropriates things of value (i.e., food) from another species and returns nothing (Cohen and Machalek 1988). In contrast, warriors protect society from possible destruction by another society and so are usually accorded great respect (warriors may also attack a weaker society, a less morally defensible use of violence). Nonetheless, there still may be some overlap between war and crime. Just as sports metaphors infuse the daily talk of men (and of fewer women), warlike motives may infuse some criminal behavior.

The young men in "Monster" Kody Scott's (under his new legal name, Shakur) *Autobiography of an L.A. Gang Member* (1994) fought gang "wars." Monster's gang faced off against a rival gang whose members were regarded as enemies; territories were staked out and claimed; and raids of reprisal were carried out into other gangs' territories. Members of a rival gang were ambushed by Monster and his gun-toting friends; some rival gang members were killed. If no military uniforms were issued and worn, if no state sanctioned this behavior, it was not altogether different from a small detachment of troops going behind enemy lines for a lighting strike. In both cases, an enemy is identified, a group of men make a raid (and train for it), and weapons are used to kill. The analogy to war actually seems closer than Gold's (1970) comparison of a delinquent gang to a "pickup" sports team. A pickup game involves teams of cooperating boys or men with some loyalty to one another. In toughly played basketball on a city hardcourt, though, no one gets killed. Whether a similarity of gang turf battles to warfare reveals a common psychological etiology or is only a metaphor is not altogether clear. However, this question must remain an open one as we consider biological influences on criminality.

The Heterogeneity of the Causes of Crime

Crime has many causes. Many different constellations of traits can predispose toward crime. Consider, for instance, the case of David Berkowitz, the infamous "Son of Sam." He terrorized New York City in the mid-1970s, sneaking up on young couples in parked cars and shooting them. He killed six people and wounded seven. The city became so terrorized that women started to dye their hair lighter colors, because of a belief that Berkowitz favored brunette women as targets. According to Berkowitz, voices spoke to him and ordered him to kill. His acts were those of a madman who can be diagnosed as a "paranoid schizophrenic." His predisposition toward murder was not a garden-variety problem of low self-control, as described by Gottfredson and Hirschi (1990). Schizophrenia is a heritable psychological disorder. A whole book could be devoted to the role of the serious heritable mental illness in crime. That is not the emphasis of this book, however; although the major psychoses can lead a person to commit heinous crimes, such traits are probably not the most common ones that contribute to the criminal disposition. Low attention span, sensation seeking, aggressiveness, and, yes, low self-control probably cover more of the population engaged in crime. Thus, these traits will be given a greater emphasis in this book.

The book also devotes little space to consideration of how intelligence might influence crime. In general, criminals score somewhat more poorly on IQ tests than noncriminals do (Hirschi and Hindelang 1977). I see low IQ as augmenting the effect of other behavioral traits rather than as a core cause of crime itself. Most individuals of low IQ are law abiding, but in everyday life, people of lower intelligence may make, on average, poorer decisions about courses of action than people of higher intelligence do; they may be less able to handle the complexity of everyday life (Gottfredson 1997). Probably everyone makes poor decisions now and then—I can recall forgetting to turn off the main water valve inside a cabin basement while turning the water on outside, resulting in a short-term gusher. Yet the inability of low-IQ persons to adequately plan for the future and their choice of less than optimal responses on a daily basis may lead to more frequent poor life decisions. For instance, someone who has trouble keeping track of his or her finances is more likely to overdraw a bank account that someone who calculates accurately. However, a person who does not care much about the future is probably in worse shape than a poor calculator. Finally, a poor calculator who does not care much about his or her future is probably in the worst shape of all—and this person comes closest to possessing a criminal disposition.

A person's characteristics do not act in isolation. Crime is the result of myriad social influences, ranging from accessibility of criminal opportunity to membership in delinquent gangs. Thus, individual traits must be viewed in a social context. Although this book emphasizes the individual level of analysis, social influences are examined in chapter 6. In summary, I am firmly of the opinion that there is not "one cause" of crime, nor just one solution for it.

Two Biological Perspectives on Crime

The biological approach to crime consists of two broad perspectives: behavioral genetics and sociobiology, or evolutionary psychology. Both seek out the roots of behavior in biology as well as in the environment, but they differ in their historical origins, primary research methods, and typical research questions.

Briefly, the nineteenth century founder of behavioral genetics was Francis Galton, an Englishman of many talents. He contributed the barometric maps used in weather forecasting to meteorology and the use of fingerprinting for individual identity to forensics. He wrote a best-selling travel book about his adventures in Africa (*The Art of Travel* 1872) and invented the correlation coefficient, a basis of modern statistics. His work on individual differences in personality and intellect led to behavioral genetics. In particular, he conducted a family study of genius to determine whether outstanding intellectual accomplishment was biologically inherited. His book on this topic, *Hereditary Genius* (1869), created a program for behavioral genetic research on intellectual ability. He also pioneered the twin and adoption study methods.

Following Galton's interest in human traits, *behavioral genetics* is the study of genetic and environmental influences on individual differences in traits in humans and nonhuman animals. People differ in myriad physical and psychological traits—from shoe size to intelligence. Any individual difference in a measurable trait is grist for the mill of a behavioral genetic study. A measurable trait is called a *phenotype,* meaning that which can be reliably observed and measured about individuals. Thus, twin and adoption studies, the mainstay methods in behavioral genetics, can be used to detect genetic influences on variations in foot length, intellectual ability, or any other observable trait.

The nineteenth-century founder of evolutionary theory was Galton's cousin, Charles Darwin. Darwin served as the naturalist and companion to Captain FitzRoy on the ship *Beagle*. The ship's journey of exploration through the Pacific led Darwin to the Galapagos Islands, off the coast of Ecuador. On these islands, he observed the varieties of finches, each with a beak best adapted to a particular food source, from thick, strong beaks for crushing tough pods to get at the nuts inside to thin, fragile beaks for picking soft seeds off the ground. He theorized, correctly, that the finches descended from one ancestral species of finch that had flown—or more likely was blown in a storm—from the mainland to the Galapagos. The radiation of the one ancestor into the great variety of finch species—now called Darwin's finches—that Darwin observed on the Galapagos Islands was part of the evidence that convinced him of the existence of an evolutionary process (Darwin 1859).

In 1975, the renowned Harvard biologist Edward O. Wilson wrote a book about the evolution of behavioral traits across animal species. He added a last chapter on the application of evolutionary theory to human behavior and coined the name *sociobiology* for this fledgling field. He argued that behavior can be understood as arising from biological evolution in that behavioral traits are adaptive—that is, traits that serve the functions of survival allow individuals to produce offspring, who themselves survive and reproduce to carry copies of their parental genes onward into future generations. Sociobiology became controversial, not in the least because Wilson imagined it swallowing up various social science disciplines, but also because of its ensuing social and political controversies. More recently, the field has come to be called *evolutionary psychology*, with a greater emphasis on how adaptation shapes thought and emotion rather than on social behaviors.

The evolutionary program of research is most concerned with the brain as an adaptive organ, shaped by evolution—much as evolution has perfected the eye to see the world, or the wing to hold a hawk aloft. This research focuses on universal behaviors, or on behaviors specific to males and females of a species that result from the adaptive problems faced by males and females over evolutionary time. This approach focuses on behaviors that affect the chances of survival and reproduction, such as aggression and altruism, and ignores those that may be a consequential domain of individual differences but not necessarily one closely related to behavioral adaptation, such as general intelligence. In terms of genes, this approach is more concerned with the effects of gene variants that are shared by all humanity and less concerned with genes that are polymorphic (i.e., that come in many forms) and so differ among individuals, such as those that determine height or eye color.

Chapters 2 and 3 consider how the behavioral genetic and evolutionary theories contribute to our understanding of crime and criminal disposition.

Levels of Biological Analysis

Reductionism is seeking the explanation of complex scientific phenomena in simpler ones. In physics, equations are used to describe physical forces that exist under ideal conditions of vacuum and no friction. In biology, the impulse patterns of a single nerve cell are analyzed, even though the brain is composed of billions of nerve cells.

Reductionism has both good and bad qualities. On one hand, few sciences would have ever advanced without it. In chemistry, for instance, understanding of chemical reactions was greatly enhanced by describing them as reactions among the limited number of elements represented in Mendelev's periodic table. In physics, Newton's laws of gravity allow plotting courses to the moon or Mars with pinpoint accuracy, although in the long run planetary orbits can become unpredictable because gravitational interactions among several planets and their moons can create chaotic motions. If science has taught us anything, it is that to understand nature: "Simplify, simplify, and simplify."

On the other hand, reductionism cannot solve all problems in science. Complexity theorists point out that by reducing phenomena to simple laws, we lose the effects of interactions at higher levels. In human affairs, predictions often fail. No one has found a surefire method of predicting the stock market's gains or losses or predicting the rise and fall of political states. No pundit predicted the rapid collapse of a dominant world power, the Soviet Union, in 1989. Although the mind is nothing more than electrochemical activity in the brain, the converse is untrue: No single neuron is the mind.

In biological reductionism, we look for specific changes in physiology that are associated with crime. Reductionism comes in softer and harder varieties. The more a single biological substrate relates to a physical or behavioral trait, the stronger the possible reductionism to a biological level of explanation. In the strongest form of causality, just one gene and the protein molecule it produces are involved. Consider a neurological disorder, Huntington's disease. The inheritance of a single copy of a defective gene, from either one's mother or father, leads inevitably to this disease in adulthood. The first symptoms are usually uncontrolled movements in the arms and legs, forgetfulness, and personality change, followed by a general mental decline and then death. The causal sequence is the inheritance of one gene to one fatal disease. This is biological determinism at its strongest, a preordained fate knowable well in advance (and as of this writing still not treatable).

If only crime were so easy. But it is not. Crime does not have one specific cause in the brain. There are degrees of biological influence on behavior, from direct determinism to none (except in the loosest sense that all behavior is biologically instated). Biological influences on crime fall somewhere between these extremes. Each biological influence is a slight nudge, pushing in the general direction of a stronger criminal disposition. The more a biological influence increases the risk of crime or a crimelike behavior and nothing else, the more likely that its influence is specific to crime. One of the interesting questions about biological influences on crime is at how many levels reductionism will work. Can we move from personality traits to individual differences in physiology? Chapter 4 covers some physiological correlates of crime. As reviewed in more detail in chapter 4, a low resting heart rate in a brief laboratory test can anticipate later criminal behavior, but it is only a moderate nudge in that direction.

Physiological differences in the brain are partly a result of the inheritance of different variants of genes. Chapter 5 examines the contribution of molecular genetics to understanding crime. The degree of genetic determination of crime depends partly on how many genes have moderate effects on the risk of crime. The fewer the number of genes, the more each gene can tell us about the biological dispositions toward crime. At this time, no one knows how many genes might be relevant and how strong their effects are. In chapter 5, I examine several single-gene effects in more detail.

Environmental Influences

Chapter 6 considers sources of environmental influence on criminal disposition and crime rates. It opens by considering peer groups as an environmental cause of crime. Peer-group members are alike in their crime rates, a resemblance that is partly a case of "birds of a feather flocking together" and partly an influence of one person on another. The discussion of peers is also a good context in which to consider a gene-to-environment correlation—that is, how people choose environments that reinforce their genetic predispositions. Family influences are considered in a context of genotype x environment interactions. The last section of the chapter deals with historical change in crime rates, which proceed at a more rapid pace than genetic change does. The historical record may reveal specific environmental and demographic influences on crime, but the complexity of historical time often clouds which new aspect of culture or demography was responsible for an increase or decrease in crime.

Chapter 7 steps into the most contentious ethical and legal issues prompted by biological discoveries about criminal disposition and by abuses of biological ideas in recent history. The chapter examines tension between medical and criminal justice models of crime. Although not widely acknowledged, medical treatments are often used with persons within the criminal justice system, especially with adolescents. Given advances in psychiatry, greater contact between the medical and justice systems is probably inevitable. Chapter 7 also covers a controversy about using biological tests to predict children's future criminal behavior, much as biological tests are used to predict some medical disorders. In the nineteenth and early twentieth centuries, the eugenics movement proposed a restriction on the reproduction of the "unfit" as a possible remedy to a host of social ills, including crime. The chapter concerns about possible misuse of biological knowledge considers crime on behalf of a revived eugenics movement. Finally, the reader is encouraged to learn more about the biological bases of criminal behavior.

References

Boyd, W. 1990. *Brazzaville Beach*. London: Sinclair-Stevenson.

Chagnon, N. A. 1988. "Life Histories, Blood Revenge, and Warfare in a Tribal Population." *Science* 239: 985–992.

Cohen, L. E. and R. Machalek. 1988. "A General Theory of Expropriative Crime: An Evolutionary Ecological Approach." *American Journal of Sociology* 94: 465–501.

Darwin, C. 1859. *On the Origin of Species by Means of Natural Selection, or the Preservation of Favoured Races in the Struggle for Life.* London: John Murray (Harvard University Press, 1975).

Galton, F. 1869. *Hereditary Genius: An Inquiry Into Its Laws and Its Consequences.* London: Macmillan (Cleveland World Publishing Co., 1962).

— 1872. *The Art of Travel.* London: John Murray.

Gold, M. 1970. *Delinquent Behavior in an American City.* Belmont, CA: Wadsworth.

Gottfredson, L. S. 1997. "Why *g* Matters: The Complexity of Everyday Life." *Intelligence* 24: 79–132.

Gottfredson, M. R. and T. Hirschi. 1990. *A General Theory of Crime.* Stanford, CA: Stanford University Press.

Hirschi, T. and M. J. Hindelang. 1977. "Intelligence and Delinquency: A Revisionist Review." *American Sociological Review* 42: 571–587.

Shakur, S. 1994. *Monster: The Autobiography of an L.A. Gang Member.* New York: Penguin Books.

Wilson, E. O. 1975. *Sociobiology: The New Synthesis.* Cambridge, MA: Harvard University Press.

Wrangham, R. and D. Peterson. 1996. *Demonic Males: Apes and the Origins of Human Violence.* New York: Houghton Mifflin. ✦

Chapter 2

The Heritability of Criminal Disposition

Humans at birth are not neutral with respect to the propensity toward committing crimes. Some individuals are more biologically predisposed toward crime than others. Indeed, as all personality traits have some physiological basis and are influenced by genes (Loehlin 1992), it would be baffling if genetic influences on crime were totally absent. The more important questions are, What in brain physiology gives some people a greater propensity toward crime, and do genetic influences interact with specific environmental ones? But before we get to these issues, we need to examine some of the evidence for genetic influences on crime. We will also look at environmental influences on crime. Although "behavior genetics" mentions only "genetics" in its name, its methods actually reveal as much about environmental influences as about genetic ones. Thus, any behavioral genetic study shows not only the extent of genetic influences, but also the types and strengths of environmental influences.

Identical Twins and Crime

Identical twins provide a means of discovering genetic influence on crime. Identical twins are called *monozygotic* (MZ) twins because both come from a single fertilized egg (*mono* = single, *zygote* = egg). This fertilized egg cell contains 23 chromosomes (the genetic material) from the mother's egg cell and another 23 from the father's sperm cell. All cells that are daughters of the fertilized egg are genetically identical. As the fertilized egg cell repeatedly divides, something goes wrong and the growing cluster of cells splits into two embryos. Each section of the embryo then continues to divide to become one of the individuals in an identical twin pair. Each twin carries exactly the same complement of genes. For this reason, a piece of skin grafted from one twin onto the other will not be rejected by the immune system. The immune system recognizes a skin graft as "self" because it comes from a genetically identical person. More rarely, an embryo splits to form a greater number of identical individuals. In the famous case of the Genain quadruplets, all suffered from the same psychiatric disorder: schizophrenia (Gottesman 1991, 125–126).

Would a set of identical quadruplets be matched for crime as well? Probably not, if by identical we require that the twins commit exactly the same crime. I doubt we will ever find an Inspector Clouseau relying on the criminal case of one identical twin to solve the crime of another. Rather, genetic influence on crime implies that when one identical twin commits many acts of the type described on self-report delinquency scales (stealing, getting into fights, lying, conning others), the other twin is also likely to commit an above-average number of such acts. Conversely, when an identical twin commits few delinquent or criminal acts, so should his or her twin. As an example, the Krays were a pair of identical twins who rose from a modest social background to dominate organized crime in England. The story of their brutal rise to power is told in the 1990 movie, *The Krays*. The case of the Han twins has been used to illustrate a pair of identical twins discordant for crime. Jeen Han was accused of having her friends tie up and hold her twin sister, Sunny, at gunpoint. However, the Abel and Cain story weakened when the police revealed that Sunny also had a criminal history (Stryker 1997).

The ideal research design for demonstrating genetic influences on crime is to study identical twins raised apart. Each twin, reared by different adoptive parents, would be exposed to a different set of environmental influences while growing up. Of course, the ideal experiment of separating twins at birth and randomly assigning them to adoptive parents is unethical and cannot be done by scientists. However, in some cases twins are inadvertently separated at birth for a variety of reasons, such as economic hardships, and are raised unknown to each other by adoptive parents or by biological relatives. Although the raised-apart design is imperfect, it could rule out genetic influences if such twins were not at all alike or could support it if they are concordant for crime.

Because separated twin pairs are rare and finding them is costly and difficult, we have some studies that are just case histories and only a few that involve multiple sets of twin pairs. One of these studies, the Minnesota Study of Separated Twins, found enough pairs for analysis and is the source for many fascinating anecdotes about separated twins (Segal 1999). For instance, one pair of reunited identical twin sisters giggled constantly and found humor in almost anything. Another pair of sisters came adorned with multiple rings across their fingers. The Jim twins both married first and second wives of the same names and built similar wooden benches around trees in their front yards. They shared woodworking as a hobby and had extensive tool rooms in their homes. Of course, some of these similarities, such as marrying women with the same name, are probably merely coincidences. Other similarities, such as using a foreign brand toothpaste with an odd taste, probably reflect genetic similarities in taste preferences. Certainly, many more behavioral similarities were found among reunited identical twin pairs than among reunited fraternal twin pairs. One exception was a pair of reunited fraternal twins with heavy tattooing all over their bodies.

A study of criminality of separated twins used one set of separated identical triplets (three possible pairings of the triplets, AB, AC, and BC) and 31 separated twin pairs (Grove et al. 1990). The twins were adults at the time they were interviewed; they were brought to the University of Minnesota from all over the country and sometimes from outside the United States. The interview involved questions used to score psychiatric disorders on the Diagnostic Manual of the American Psychiatric Association (DSM III). In this study, a more continuous score was created by summing the number of symptoms of both childhood and adult "antisocial personality disorder." Committing crimes was taken as evidence of both disorders, as was irresponsible behaviors such as going into debt and cheating on others. The estimate of genetic influence on antisocial personality symptoms was .28 for adult symptoms (range .00 to .52) and .45 for childhood symptoms (.14 to .62). The technical term for these estimates is *heritability*, which is discussed in the following section. We can be 95 percent confident that the true level of genetic influence lies within the ranges given. Because the range of genetic influence on childhood and adult antisocial personality overlaps, we cannot claim that one genetic influence is stronger than the other. The range for the adult symptoms also included zero as an extreme boundary, but we will see other evidence in this chapter that makes zero an unreasonable value for genetic influence. The lack of precision in these estimates is frustrating but expected because the sample size was only 34 pairs. A clear implication, though, is that reared-apart identical twins show some similarity, reflecting genetic influence, for symptoms of antisocial personality disorder. Childhood and adult symptoms were also associated. Although some bias may come from the retrospective nature of these self-reports—adults remembering their childhood and adult symptoms—we will also see later in this chapter that adult crime has childhood precursors in the behavioral disorders of childhood. From the analysis of the separated twins, the study also revealed that the genetic correlation of the childhood and adult symptoms was .61. In other words, common genes influenced criminal symptoms in both the childhood and adult periods.

How to Interpret Heritability Coefficients

Genetic influence is often expressed in terms of a *heritability coefficient.* This number gives a quantitative value for the strength of genetic influence, but it is often confusing to student and practitioner alike. The heritability coefficient was invented to help animal breeders determine which traits would respond most strongly to artificial selection for economically desirable characteristics. The greater the heritability, the faster that selective breeding can change a trait, such as coat color or temperament in dogs. For instance, it is faster to breed cattle for percentage of meat than for milk production. Although in human genetics no breeding programs are planned, the coefficient is still used to express the strength of a genetic influence.

The possible values of heritability, which is given the mathematical symbol h^2, range from 0 to 1.0. Intuitively, heritability represents the percentage of individual differences in a trait accounted for by genetic differences among individuals. One way to think about this concept is in terms of gene substitution: The simple replacement of one variant of a gene by another leads to changes in a trait. Such a substitution makes one person blue eyed and another brown eyed. The heritability of eye color is nearly 100 percent because nearly all the individual differences—colored contact lens aside—arise from one gene variant being substituted for another. A French person and a Chinese person differ in many genes affecting physical traits, but one speaks the language of lovers and the other speaks the language of the Golden Kingdom because of their rearing. Thus, the heritability of language is 0 percent. Height has a heritability of about .90; that is, 90 percent of the individual differences in height are due to genetic variation.

An analogy may help you understand genetic influences. A friend of mine once gave a dinner party where she served a delicious-looking pecan pie. However, her guests made faces of disgust after the first bite. Salt had accidentally been substituted for sugar when the pie was made, and the salt had ruined the pie's taste. The "trait" here is the taste of the pie; in behavioral genetics terminology, any observable trait is called a *phenotype*—something that can be measured, in this case, by the sensitive human palate. The genetic makeup of the pie—its *genotype*—was either one gene variant (salt) or another (sugar). The "heritability" of pecan pie taste from this change in ingredients is about 100 percent. Notice that to make this observation, we need not have any training in chemistry. We can taste the effect of the substitution of ingredients without knowing how salt affects the baking of a pie. Indeed, brewers made perfectly excellent beers long before theoretical chemistry made its appearance! Thus, the effects of genes can be inferred without knowing their physiological pathways or how they may interact in development with other genes. This knowledge is highly desirable, however.

Now that the idea of heritability is clearer, the question still remains: How are we to interpret a heritability of .10, .40, or .80? A heritability of .10 means that 10 percent of the phenotypic variation is explained by variation of gene variants. To a plant breeder, this is a fairly disappointing figure, implying that changing an economically valued trait in the plant species would take many generations and be quite costly. In social science, an index of the strength of relationship between two variables is the correlation coefficient, r. A correlation coefficient of 0 indicates no association between two variables whereas $r = 1$ indicates a perfect association. When a variable Y is predicated from X, a correlation of .50 would explain 25 percent of the variation in Y (i.e., $r^2 = .25$). To social scientists, whose variables typically explain roughly 10 percent of variation, a heritability of 10 percent is roughly equivalent to the strength of influence typically found for many environmental influences, such as parental discipline styles (i.e., $r = .30$, or $r^2 = 9$ percent of the variance). The statistician Cohen gave a rough rule of thumb for treatment outcome studies: explaining 1 percent ($r = .10$), 9 percent ($r = .30$), and 25 percent ($r = .50$) of the variance were small, moderate, and large effect sizes (McCartney and Rosenthal 2000). Another measure of effect size is *d*, the difference between two groups in standard deviation units. For example, if a treatment raised a group of children's average IQ by 15 points (1 standard deviation), the *d* value is 1.0. When talking about effect size, I usually convert group mean differences (i.e., *d* values) into correlation coefficients. Thus, the 15-point IQ gain is equivalent to a correlation coefficient of $r = .45$, or 20 percent of the variance.

By Cohen's rule of thumb, most genetic influences on behavioral characteristics would be strong ones. My own view is that heritabilities of .10 and above tell us to pay attention to genetic influences and biology. The exact heritability is less important than finding ways in which biological information can help us understand the origins of criminality and use that information in both prevention and treatment, ideas that are taken up in later chapters.

Inferring Genetic Influence on Behavioral Characteristics

There are two ways to infer genetic influence on behavioral traits. One is to genotype people for molecular genetic markers and then compare the trait means of people who differ in the marker. A person is genotyped when we know the specific genetic variants that he or she carries. For example, many people know their blood types. Blood type O is genotype OO because genes come in pairs. Blood type B is genotype BB or genotype BO because O is recessive to B. Now, if people of blood type OO had a higher mean level of self-report delinquency than those of blood type BB or BO, an association would exist between genotype and phenotype–in this case, between blood type and criminality. Such an association has never been found, however. In chapter 5, we consider in greater detail evidence for an effect of specific genotypes on criminality and look at genes that are more likely to influence behavioral traits than blood type gene variants.

Another way to infer genetic influence is to look for phenotypic resemblance in biological relatives. The logic of this method is fairly simple, because genetic relatives share more gene variants than unrelated people do. That is why people in an extended family look alike;

they should also be more alike in their behavior. Genetic relatedness is quantified as *R*, a coefficient of genetic relatedness that ranges from 0 to 1.0. By definition, this is the proportion of genes shared by two relatives who are identical by biological descent from common ancestors. In their genetically influenced behaviors, identical twins with a genetic relatedness of $R = 1.0$ should be more alike than fraternal twins, who have a relatedness of $R = .50$. Biological full siblings ($R = 0.50$) should be more alike than biological half-siblings ($R = .25$). Half-siblings, in their turn, should be more alike than adoptive siblings ($R = 0$) or an adoptive child paired with a biological child of the same adoptive parents ($R = 0$).

The Classic Twin Study Design: Genetic Influences

This logic has led to the classical twin design of comparing the phenotypic resemblance of fraternal and identical twins. The genetic expectation is that identical twins ($R = 1.0$) will be twice as similar as fraternal twins ($R = .50$). This does not mean that identical twins yield a phenotypic correlation of 1.0 and fraternal twins .50. The ratio is preserved if the identical twins correlate .18 and the fraternal twins .09. One reason that twins do not resemble each other as strongly as they could is that characteristics are measured imperfectly. For example, identical twins correlate about .90 for height. Suppose we let two 9-year-old research assistants, one for each twin, measure their heights with an elastic tape measure. This procedure could introduce errors of measurement, and the height correlation on twin pairs would undoubtedly fall to something well below .90. Poor measurements can make twins look less alike than they really are. Real environmental influences can also decrease twins' resemblance, a topic discussed further below.

Behavioral geneticists have devoted considerable effort to evaluating several assumptions of the classic twin study (Rowe 1994). These assumptions are the "equal environments assumption" and the "unbiased by appearance" assumption. For most behavioral characteristics, these assumptions seem to be satisfied. The picture for criminality, however, is more complex.

The "unbiased by appearance" assumption refers to the view that the greater resemblance of identical twins is not simply a matter of their looking alike. Appearance certainly influences some behavioral characteristics; for instance, attractive teenage boys and girls usually get more dates on weekends. But it does not influence many other characteristics. For example, personality traits and IQ only correlate weakly, or not at all, with physical appearance. So the greater appearance similarity of identical twins makes them only trivially, or not at all, more alike in personality and intellect. Consider as examples that both Clyde (of Bonnie and Clyde) and Marilyn Monroe possessed exceptional physical attractiveness, but that appearance guaranteed neither moral goodness nor happiness.

In the field of criminology, the view that appearance strongly determined criminal disposition was popular under phrenology in the 1800s and early 1900s (Lombroso and Lombroso 1972). Criminals were said to possess atavistic (primitive) features such as big brow ridges and small foreheads that pointed to their closer connection with humanity's apelike ancestors. Although some physical characteristics, such as a greater muscularity, remain linked with criminality, the facial features described by phrenologists were found to be unassociated with either criminal convictions or imprisonment in many studies, some undertaken in the 1800s. Negative empirical evidence has convinced criminologists to abandon phrenology as an explanation of crime. By the same token, criminologists cannot claim that physical appearance is what drives identical twins' resemblance for crime.

The equal environments assumption is also important for drawing inferences about environmental influence from twin studies. This assumption is that identical and fraternal twins are treated alike in ways that influence a characteristic. Some treatments of identical and fraternal twins are similar. For example, radon gas influences cancer risks. In some homes, radon levels are high, so twin children are both exposed to high levels of radiation, whereas in other homes, little radon gas is present and the risk to either twin is low. There is no reason to think, however, that identical twins are more matched in their exposure to radon gas than fraternal twins are. Thus, "exposure to radon" would satisfy the equal environments assumption of the twin method.

In another instance, treatments are clearly unequal: Identical twins, who often look very cute sitting beside each other in matching outfits, are dressed alike by their parents and paraded before the world more often than fraternal twins . Does this greater similarity of treatment of identical twins violate the assumption? Only if the treatment also influences the phenotype under study. No one would suggest that similar outfits make twins more alike for their cancer risk. Thus, this apparent violation is not a violation if the phenotype is cancer rates. What about IQ? If stylish clothes somehow made people smarter than unstylish ones, then "dressed alike" could be a violation of the assumption for IQ. Most people do not believe this, however. If clothing styles really worked to change IQ, ambitious parents would be unrelenting in dressing their children "for success."

Behavioral geneticists have devoted considerable effort to evaluating the "equal environments" assumption (Rowe 1994, 42–48). For many phenotypes, leveling this criticism at twins studies has been a red herring—of little real merit, but unfortunately effective, because by repetition many people have come to believe it (without much serious reflection on their part).

Criminality poses an exception to the consistent support of the equal environments assumption. Two kinds of violations of the assumption occur when crime is the phenotype. The first is that delinquency, and often adult crime as well, tends to be a group phenomenon. Among the people chosen as "partners in crime" are cotwins, and for nontwin siblings, their brothers and sisters (Rowe 1983). Thus, there is a statistical bias toward greater similarity of both kinds of twins because criminal acts committed jointly add to the total count of acts for both individuals in a twin pair. Another violation is that identical twins have more social contact with each other than fraternal twins do; they are more likely to spend time together and to have the same friends. To some extent, these preferences are genetically driven. Identical twins are more likely to have similar personalities and interests than fraternal twins because they are genetically alike individuals (as has been confirmed in studies of twins raised apart—see Bouchard et al. 1990; Loehlin 1992). Nonetheless, because they spend more time together and share more friends, they also have a greater opportunity to influence each other or be influenced by their band of companions. These violations imply that estimates of heritability from twin studies are probably biased upward. On the other hand, the violation is equally interesting as evidence for a type of peer-environmental influence on crime.

Environmental Influences

Studies of twins and adoptive children cannot avoid revealing environmental influences on behavior. Adoptive children are an ideal population in which to discover family environmental influences, because on average adoptees grow up with parents with whom they share no genes. They may coincidently share a genetic trait with their adoptive parents, such as eye color, but more typically they will not. For example, if you examined a large number of European-heritage adoptive parents and adoptive children, some of the blue-eyed adoptive parents would have brown-eyed children because the adoptive children had brown-eyed biological parents. Conversely, some of the brown-eyed adoptive parents would have blue-eyed adoptive children because again the child had a different biological heritage. Overall, there would be no more matches than chance allows. Thus, knowing the eye color of the European-heritage adoptive parents, one could not make a prediction of the eye color of their European-heritage adoptive children.

In biological families, children and parents show some resemblance for eye color because of their shared genes—the genes that a child inherits directly from a parent. Of course, identical twins who are perfect genetic matches of each other are almost always alike in eye color. A rare exception comes from somatic (body cell) mutations that may change one twin's eye color. The same logic applies to other genes, even ones of unknown function. Biological parents and children will share these genes on average; adoptive parent and child will not. Thus, when a behavioral resemblance is found between an adoptive child and his or her adoptive parent, it strengthens the case for an environmental influence on the particular behavior. Not surprisingly, adoptive children often adopt the religion in which they are raised, which they learn by example and instruction from their parents' church. On the other hand, little family environmental influence exists on obesity. Obese adoptive parents are equally likely to have thin or fat adoptive children. Stereotypically, fat people are thought to gobble down potato chips, french fries, and burgers. Against the common sense that bad eating habits (to the extent they actually exist) would influence children's weight, a lack of parental influence on obesity is a robust result. Genes appear to be the paramount influence on weight (Stunkard et al. 1986).

A twin study can also show environmental influence. For example, twins may exhibit little resemblance for one characteristic—left versus right handedness—regardless of whether they are identical or fraternal. Table 2.1 presents the generally low handedness correlations in both identical and fraternal twin pairs (Loehlin and Nichols

1976). Handedness can be reliably measured and is a persisting characteristic, as you can discover by trying to write with your nondominant hand. Many environmental influences affect handedness that twins do not share, influences that may make one twin a lefty and the other a righty and thus cannot contribute to twins' similarity. Behavior genetic theories of handedness must invoke a process of genotype x environment interaction to explain these data (their details are beyond our topic, but the interested reader can consult Corballis 1997).

Table 2.1
The Surprising Dissimilarity of Identical and Fraternal Twins' Tendency Toward Left Handedness

Group	*N*	Correlation
Identical twins	428	.02
Fraternal twins	268	.05

Note: The correlations are averaged, twin samples 1 and 2, from the original report.
Source: Laland et al. 1995.

Other characteristics correlate nearly as highly for fraternal as for identical twins. In adult twins, church attendance is one such characteristic (Loehlin 1993). Correlation coefficients, which give a quantitative measure of similarity (0 = not at all alike to 1.0 = perfectly alike), indicate that fraternal twins are more alike in church attendance than would be expected genetically. This finding implies some source of twin similarity, something more than shared genes; it could be the family environment or other influences tied to growing up together. Certainly, many families make strong efforts to inculcate religious beliefs, and by their teaching and example they may create twin pairs' resemblance. A characteristic for which fraternal twins correlate, say .40, and identical twins correlate by the same amount, would rule out genetic influence—unless it is just a chance result of a small sample size—and rule in some kind of environmental influence that makes children who grow up together behaviorally alike.

Shared and Nonshared Environmental Influences

Environmental influences are generally classified into two types: shared and unshared. *Shared* influences are those that result in some common exposure to siblings and that influence them similarly. Consider some extreme households that stereotypically might influence children's development. In Homer's household (borrowed shamelessly from Homer Simpson of TV cartoon fame) the favorite paternal activities are watching TV, guzzling beer, scarfing up donuts, and avoiding work. In Aristotle's household, the favorite paternal activities are reading, talking about items in the news, playing golf, and sipping Chardonnay wine (an Australian label). Now, many people would predict different outcomes for children in these two households—a college-bound track for Aristotle's child and a vocational track for Homer's son. Because differences between families are so impressive, family environments can be expected to make children from different families unlike but siblings from the same household alike.

Table 2.2

Examples of Shared and Nonshared Environmental Influences

Shared Influences	Nonshared Influences
Social class[1]	Parents treat siblings differently
Parental religiosity	Developmental events to the fetus[2]
Global parental warmth	Different teachers
Parental vocabulary level	Different peer groups
Neighborhood disorganization	Stressful daily life experiences

1. Social class can also contribute to sibling differences—for instance, if two siblings were born eight years apart and the family went from rags to riches between the birth of the first and second child. The total shared influence is the sum of all impacts of specific environmental experiences that are common to siblings; a particular experience might contribute partly to the total shared variation and partly to the unshared part.

2. These environments could be "biological ones," such as when one child but not the other is exposed to a virus during fetal development. Behavioral geneticists use the word "environment" to refer to everything that is not genetic.

Nonshared environmental influences are those that operate to make siblings (or parent-child pairs) dissimilar. Even identical twins are not exactly alike in their physical traits, such as their facial features and teeth alignments. Such differences can arise because of the complexities of in utero development, when a variety of forces, from hormone levels to nutrition, impinge on the developmental pathways. In the developing embryo, the pace of cell division is astronomical—and it will never occur in exactly the same way twice. In light of the complexities of development, it is amazing that identical twins are as similar as they are. Other sources of dissimilarity can be unique experiences with teachers, peer groups that encourage different behaviors, and differential parental treatments. A caution is in order here, however. Differential parental treatments are nonshared environmental influences if they provoke different behaviors in children. On the other hand, if a hyperactive child elicits harsher parental discipline than a more easygoing brother or sister, the differential treatment is not an environmental influence on the child—just the opposite: The child has molded parental behavior. Table 2.2 lists potential shared and nonshared environmental influences. They are *potential* influences because one must insure that they actually cause variation in a particular behavioral trait.

Estimating Genetic and Environmental Influences in Behavioral Genetic Research Designs

For criminal behavior, how does one estimate heritability (h^2), shared environmental influences (c^2), and nonshared environmental influences (e^2)? I have already discussed two approaches: looking at twins raised apart and at the classic twin design that uses both identical and fraternal twins. Table 2.3 summarizes these methods, plus a couple of other possibilities. In behavioral genetics, complex statistics are often used to arrive at the estimates of h^2, c^2, and e^2. However, these mathematical methods do no more than extract information from the observed resemblances of biological relatives. Thus, consider some of the scenarios in Table 2.3. Let us assume that for any group of relatives, we have sampled 550 pairs and given them a self-report measure of criminality. The scale would have questions such as "Have you stolen a car?" and "Have you illegally carried a weapon?" The correlation coefficient that varies from 0 (not at all alike) to 1.0 (perfectly alike) indexes the behavioral similarity of the relatives.

In Example 1, both identical and fraternal twins are highly alike. Genetic influences are ruled out because identical twins are not *more* alike than fraternal twins. Common experiences make the twins alike—.56 indicates a good deal more sibling resemblance than 0! So the shared environmental effect is $c^2 = .56$. The remainder is the nonshared environmental effect, plus any measurement errors: $e^2 = .44$.

Table 2.3
Examples of Hypothetical Outcomes From Behavioral Genetic Studies of Self-Report Crime

Groups	Correlation	Influence
Example 1		
Identical twins reared together	.56	Shared environment and nonshared environment
Fraternal twins reared together	.56	
Example 2		
Identical twins reared together	.56	Heredity, shared environment, and nonshared environment
Fraternal twins reared together	.40	
Example 3		
Adoptive parent-adoptive child	.00	Heredity and nonshared environment
Adoptive parent-biological child	.33	
Example 4		
Unrelated adoptive siblings	.27	Shared environment and nonshared environment

In Example 2, the numbers are more complex. Some genetic influence exists because the identical twins are more alike than the fraternal twins. Some nonshared environmental influences exist because twins are not perfectly (1.0) alike. From these correlations, the actual estimates are $h^2 = .32$, $c^2 = .24$, and $e^2 = .44$.

Example 3 is an adoption study. The pattern of associations fits the expectations of a hypothesis of genetic influence. Adopted-away children resemble their biological parents but not their adopted parents. The estimate of genetic influence from this example is $h^2 = .66$. You might ask, why not .33, the value of the parent-child correlation? The answer is that parents and children share 50 percent of their genes, not 100 percent of them. Think of how parents and children can also differ in weight, height, complexion, and hair and eye color, as well as be somewhat alike. Thus, to compensate for the lack of 100 percent shared genes, the parent-child correlation is doubled to estimate heritability. The nonshared environmental effect is .44.

In Example 4, on the other hand, we have biologically unrelated siblings reared in the same family. Such families are created when an adoptive family adopts a second child. In the United States, when the first child is a boy, the second adoptive child is often a girl because adoptive parents can make their family balanced by choice. When these adoptive siblings are alike, it is not because of genetic relatedness because they have none, except for one caveat: Adoption agencies may give parents adoptive children who match them on some characteristic, such as social class or race, that could create biological resemblance of adoptive siblings. But in most practical cases, this bias is not very great. Let's assume that in our hypothetical example, the adoptive placement effect was zero. Then the shared environment is .27, equal to the sibling correlation. The nonshared effect is .73.

These examples illustrate a couple of principles. One is that there is more than one way to demonstrate genetic influence; study designs can include twins, adoptive children, or kin groups not even covered in Table 2.3 (for instance, half-siblings). Another is that each study design has its own particular pitfalls and strengths. As mentioned above, twins can be partners in crime, which tends to make them more alike than they would otherwise be. However, this limitation does not fault an adoptive design, as the biological parent is not in a position to influence socially an adopted-away child, especially in the closed adoptions (i.e., no contact between the adoptive and biological parents) that occurred in the past.

You do not need to be an expert in behavioral genetics to have an understanding of the general logic of its research designs. Such an understanding can help you evaluate the results of a specific study. Also, it should be clear that no single study is either perfect or definitive. A reason for accepting some genetic influence on individuals' propensity toward crime is not that one study found identical twins to be more alike than fraternal twins—which might be partly exaggerated by identical twins who committed offenses together—but because the weight of evidence from a variety of kinds of studies points this way. In the next section of this chapter, I survey some findings that support a genetic influence on criminality.

Mednick's Classic Adoption Study of Crime

Denmark is a small nation nestled against the cold and harsh North Sea. Eighty-six percent of Danes live in urban areas. The country is renowned for the fairy tales of Hans Christian Andersen and, at least to adoption researchers, for its system of excellent population records. In the 1950s, Sarnoff Mednick capitalized on this fact to locate the criminal records of adoptive children (then adults), their adoptive parents, and their biological parents. His question was simple: Do criminal records for a biological parent increase the likelihood of crime in his or her adopted-away offspring?

Mednick and colleagues' results on 14,487 adoptive children were published in *Science* in 1984. He found an increase in the rate of crime in the adopted-way offspring of criminal biological parents:

> If neither the biological nor the adoptive parents are convicted, 13.5 percent of the sons are convicted. If the adoptive parents are convicted and the biological parents are not, this figures rises only to 14.7 percent. However, if the adoptive parents are not convicted and the biological parents are, 20.0 percent of the sons are convicted. If the adoptive parents as well as the biological parents are convicted, then 24.5 percent of the sons are convicted. These data favor the assumption of a partial genetic etiology. (Mednick, Gabrielli, and Hutchings 1984, 892)

Another telling observation was a "dose dependent" relationship between crime in the biological parent and the adopted child. Presumably, a person with a longer string of convictions, and more serious ones, would carry a stronger dose of genetic disposition than someone who commits fewer crimes. Thus, more of the offspring should be affected, and affected more severely, than the offspring of biological fathers with fewer convictions. For this reason, Mednick divided the sample according to the level of biological parents' convictions.

His results appear in Figure 2.1, a bar graph of the relationship of the biological fathers' convictions to those of their adopted-away offspring. The fathers are grouped by four levels of convictions: 0, 1, 2, ≥ 3. Each bar has shading according to the children's number of convictions. As predicted, more convictions occurred among the children as the number of convictions of their biological fathers increased from zero to ≥ 3. A group of offspring with three or more convictions, who had chronically criminal fathers, consisted of 37 chronically criminal individuals; although they were a mere 1 percent of the total sample, they accounted for a remarkable 30 percent of the recorded convictions. Fortunately for Danish society, in all categories most offspring were never convicted of a crime. Genetic influence may confer a risk of criminal behavior, but it also interacts with myriad environmental influences.

Figure 2.1

Adoptive Children Percentage Convictions by Convictions of Their Biological Fathers

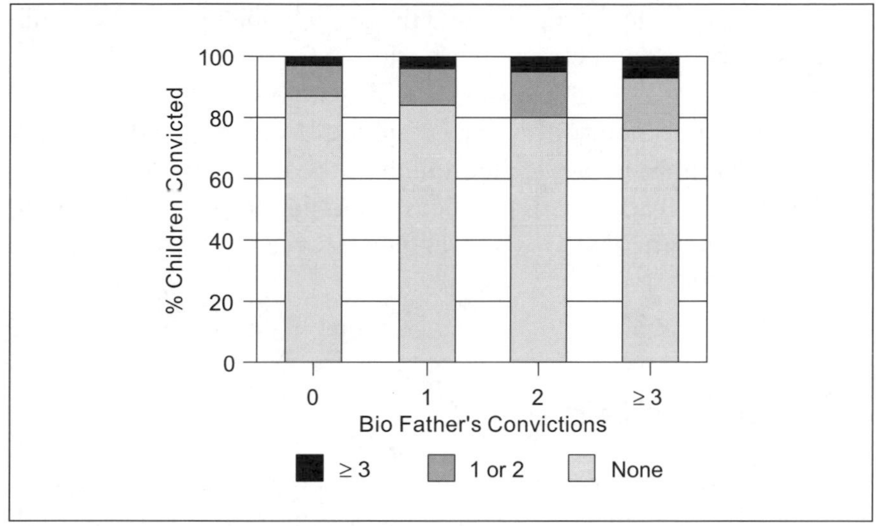

Source: Data from Mednick et al. 1984.

Mike Gottfredson and Travis Hirschi made a strong attack on Mednick's adoption study in their highly praised book, *A General Theory of Crime* (1990). They compared Mednick's statistics with an earlier finding of the relationship between parental criminality and offspring's arrest rates in a sample drawn from the city of Copenhagen. They tried to estimate the rate of criminality outside of Copenhagen by subtracting a table of within Copenhagen *arrest* rates from one of *all* Denmark *conviction* rates. This "apples minus oranges" subtraction, however, is unlikely to yield interpretable findings. In an unpublished response to his critics, Mednick mentioned this error and other mistakes made in Gottfredson and Hirschi's post hoc analysis (Mednick, personal communication). Thus, I distrust Gottfredson and Hirschi's conclusion that genetic influences on criminal behavior were absent in adoptive children in the rural areas of Denmark. Other adoptive studies done in Sweden and in the United States also support a genetic transmission of criminal disposition (e.g., Bohman et al. 1982; Cloninger et al. 1982; Cadoret et al. 1995; Rowe, Almeida, and Jacobson 1999).

Nevertheless, Gottfredson and Hirschi's approach raises the interesting point that heritability could change in different places. Parents and teachers may be more observant of children's behavior in relatively unpopulated rural areas than in the city. Their greater social control could deter criminal acts. In the city, more targets for crime may exist, and the level of policing is probably higher. Even if two children were matched in criminal disposition—for instance on a trait of "low self-control" that features prominently in Gottfredson and Hirschi's general theory of crime—they could well commit different numbers of crimes in one location than in the other, and have different likelihoods of apprehension. Ideas about genotype x environmental interactions are always worth exploring, and I return to them in chapter 6.

Twin Studies of Criminal Tendencies

Twin studies of self-report criminal acts and official arrest and conviction data have been conducted since the 1920s. These studies make a nice transition to thinking about criminality from a developmental perspective, because they highlight how the mix of genetic and environmental influences may change with age. As reviewed by DiLalla and Gottesman (1990), twin studies of delinquency in adolescence show little genetic influence. One measure of twin similarity is the twin concordance. One twin is picked who has a record of delinquency with the police or courts. Criminal records on the twin's brother or sister are then searched, and a pair is deemed concordant if both twins have criminal records. They are discordant if only one of the pair had a criminal record. In six small studies, the concordances were 87 percent for identical twins and 72 percent for fraternal twins, only a slight difference. When the same analysis was applied to adult criminality, the concordance rates differed dramatically: In an average of nine studies, the concordances were 51 percent in identical twins and 22 percent in fraternal twins, a marked difference. In my own twin study of self-reported delinquency (Rowe 1983), I estimated that 38 percent of the individual differences in delinquency were heritable, that 28 percent were due to shared environment, and that 34 percent were due to nonshared environment. Environmental sources of influence, shared by both kinds of twins, influences individual differences in delinquency.

The Developmental Perspective

The idea of a stronger genetic influence on adult than on adolescent criminality, and on more serious than on more minor deviance, is intuitively appealing. Among boys, minor violations of the law and parental expectations are common, especially when self-reported delinquency scales indict teenagers for such "offenses" as lying to their parents and staying out past curfew. These items do belong in delinquency questionnaires, however, because they are statistically associated with more serious types of crime. Their prevalences can be vastly different, though. Some 50 to 60 percent of youths lie to their parents—do we really believe those who claim complete honesty?—but only a few percent assault someone and inflict serious injury. It would seem that a criminal disposition should be rare in a population, but if 60 percent of male adolescents are "afflicted," perhaps we should examine the genetics of "normality"!

Another reason for intuitively suspecting a heterogeneity of causation—a fancy way of saying that two people who score 20 on a self-reported delinquency scale may have arrived at their scores through different life histories—is that peers can encourage delinquency, especially among boys. Gold (1970) compared a delinquent group of boys to a pickup sports team. Boys egg each other along on the basketball court, and they may do the same thing for crimes that are sometimes committed more in the spirit of a prank than of true hostile intent.

Moffitt (1993) recognized this distinction in her theory of *adolescence-limited* (AL) versus *life-course-persistent* (LCP) delinquency. According to Moffitt, the adolescent-limited delinquency variety grows out of a desire for adolescents to achieve adult maturity and is highly encouraged by supportive peers. The adolescence-limited delinquents are socially mimicking the delinquent behaviors of the supposedly more mature life-course-persistent delinquents (described below). I can understand how a 15-year-old might want to drive a Corvette and hang a hot date on his arm (the focus is on boys because Moffitt's theory is implicitly one of boys' delinquency).

However, as Judy Harris (1995) quipped, if adolescent boys really wanted a head start on adult maturity, they would practice figuring out their income tax. My point is that only some forms of delinquency—such as drinking alcoholic beverages and sexual intercourse—may presage later adulthood. A lovers' triangle leading to a physical fight is sanctioned neither in adolescence nor in adulthood, nor would other serious forms of crime be. Thus, my view is that there is something more to these typically adolescent forms of deviance than wanting to obtain adult maturity. I agree with Moffitt that delinquency is often peer-encouraged and that many adolescence-limited delinquent boys will later desist from criminality. Chapter 3 provides another explanation for the high prevalence of crime during adolescence in the intense sexual competition between males that peaks during this age, before most boys and girls have chosen their romantic partners (Kanazawa and Still 2000). According to Moffitt, genetically determined characteristics make little contribution to the adolescence-limited form of delinquency.

Life-course-persistent delinquency, in contrast, is suggested to have strong biological roots, including predisposing genes. Moffitt gives a useful method for distinguishing the two types of delinquency by looking at childhood antecedents. The life-course-persistent delinquent was antisocial in childhood, and such behavior has merely continued, and perhaps worsened, as he has grown older. In particular, the life-course-persistent delinquent exhibits various indicators of poor mental health, such as heritable psychiatric disorders. As a child, this boy would receive psychiatric diagnoses such as attention-deficit hyperactivity disorder (ADHD), oppositional defiant disorder (ODD), or conduct disorder (CD). He would score poorly on tests that assess the functioning of higher mental abilities, such as planning. He would also present with symptoms of low impulse control, harking back to the "low self-control" idea so central in Gottffredson and Hirschi's general theory of crime.

Moffitt made a sharp, categorical distinction between the two kinds of delinquents; she pigeonholed adolescents into one category or the other. In genetics, discontinuous categories correspond to well-known Mendelian principles. Gregor Mendel, in his first studies of the mechanisms of inheritance, used the traits of pea plants such as yellow pods versus green pods or smooth pods versus wrinkled pods. Mendel's fascination with pea plants was fortuitous because their traits are truly categorical and determined by single genes, like human blood groups. Pea pods don't exist that are yellowishly green; they are either yellow or green. If Mendel had chosen plant characteristics that are not determined by a single gene, his inferences about heredity would have gone awry. A clever cartoon shows Mendel serving peas to the other monks in his Czeck Republic monastery, with the caption, "Brother Mendel, not peas again."

Whether two kinds of people exist, AL and LCP delinquents, is a question ultimately answerable by research. However, my hunch is that it is better to consider these types as part of a continuum, with extreme conformity and compliance to social norms at one end and the most serious LCP delinquency at the other. Certainly, the genetic influences on these types would lie on a continuum because surely multiple genes are involved—maybe even hundreds of genes. For a simple reason of genetic combinations, multiple gene effects form the bell-shaped distribution of the normal curve. Thus, someone with moderate delinquency probably has some childhood symptoms, but fewer than the serious life-course-persistent delinquent. Even if the greater genetic risk in a moderately delinquent adolescent is not apparent in childhood behaviors, it may still be there. A number of genetic traits are called *threshold traits* because the genetic risk is not observable as a developmental abnormality until some threshold level is crossed. Unlike Mendel's smooth and wrinkled pea pods, complex characteristics do not arise from simple, categorical effects.

Moffitt's dichotomy can nonetheless be used to explain the observation of changing genetic effects on crime, with these effects often found to be weaker in adolescence than in adulthood. In adolescence, the percentage of all boys who are delinquent increases because adolescent-limited delinquents begin to offend. Many of adolescent-onset delinquents lack a strong genetic disposition toward crime. Thus, the overall heritability of crime decreases. This change does not mean that genes play no part in the adolescent onset. Just as boys can first grow beards in adolescence, they are beginning to respond to sexual desires and other motives that put them in conflict with authority, parental and otherwise. But these genetic effects are shared widely across the population. With greater experience and maturity—and perhaps with the completion of the brain's maturation in the late teens—these adolescence-limited delinquent boys will desist from crime and enter into marriage, work, and careers. However, the boys with stronger criminal dispositions, the life-course-persistent delinquents, will continue to offend and to commit other acts (such as wife abuse) that are criminal but that often escape detection by the criminal justice system. Their behavior is highly heritable, so the contrast between the law-abiding adults and criminals would have a strong genetic origin.

Box 2.1

When Are Children Most Aggressive?

The notion that children learn aggression is prevalent in American society. Social learning theorist Albert Bandura asserted, "People are not born with preformed repertories of aggressive behavior; they must learn them one way or another" (cited in Tremblay et al. 1999); the French philosopher Rousseau held that people are born without original sin in the human heart.

An age of innocence seems naive, however, based on the actual age-course of physically aggressive behavior (e.g., pushing, kicking, hitting) (Tremblay et al. 1999). The percentage of children exhibiting these behaviors jumps from near zero at 10 months of age to a sizable minority at 17 months: 48 percent pushing, 24 percent kicking, and 15 percent hitting. At a chronological age when children have watched little violent television, they are already aggressive! Fortunately, babies' limits of strength and coordination mean that they cannot inflict much bodily harm on their victims and no police department would prosecute them for assault. Yet, as in the case of nonhuman primates, aggressive actions that exist from an early age may foreshadow violent behavior later in life.

Another surprise is that physical aggression actually declines in childhood. Tremblay's research team followed another group of children from age 6 to 16 years. As shown in Figure 2.2, the mean number of aggressive acts were stable over the preschool period and then declined rapidly from age 10 onward. Nagin and Tremblay (1999) did not find any group of children who could be called "late-bloomers" for aggression—i.e., all the boys who exhibited physical aggression in midadolescence had some childhood history of the same behavior. Parents may be encouraged, though, because many children whose aggression appeared in childhood had desisted in the behavior by midadolescence.

Broadly defined aggression is moderately heritable ($h^2 \sim .50$) (Miles and Carey 1997). Like intelligence, it is a highly stable trait in individuals, with highly aggressive children tending to remain more aggressive than their peers even while all children decline in their average level of aggression (Loeber and Hay 1997; Loeber et al. 2000). Aggression is a core trait in the syndrome of deviant behaviors because more-aggressive adolescents are also more likely to commit burglary and other nonaggressive crimes. Finally, aggression may be a part of human nature; rather than a behavior that needs to be learned, it may be one that needs to be curbed from an early age.

Figure 2.2

Boys' Teacher-Rated Physical Aggression From Age 6 to 15 Years

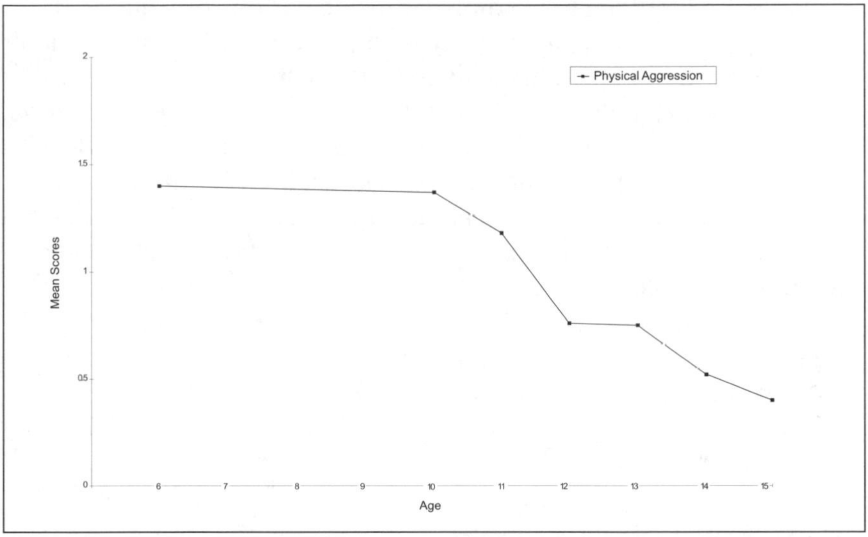

Source: Reprinted from Tremblay, R. E., C. Japel, D. Perusse, P. McDuff, M. Boivin, M. Zoccolillo, and J. Montplaisir. 1999. "The Search for the Age of 'Onset' of Physical Aggression: Rousseau and Bandura Revisited." *Criminal Behavior and Mental Health* 9, 8–23. Copyright © Whurr Publishers, Ltd. Reprinted by permission.

Psychiatric Disorders and Criminality

The field of psychiatric genetics also has learned much about the genetics of behavior disorders related to delinquency and adult criminality. Psychiatric genetics employs all the methods of behavioral genetics, but with a focus on particular psychiatric disorders (Faraone, Tsuang, and Tsuang 1999). A psychiatric disorder is usually defined using the *Diagnostic and Statistical Manual* (DSM-IV) of the American Psychiatric Association. Each disorder is defined by the presence of a certain number of symptoms, usually behaviors but sometimes physical complaints (such as lack of sleep). The severity, duration, or age of onset for a symptom may be important for a diagnosis. Although this use of systematic criteria has improved the diagnosis of psychiatric disorders, the diagnostic process is still as much art as science; thus, errors of diagnosis and disagreements between psychiatrists do occur.

In childhood, three diagnoses are most predictive of later criminal behavior: attention deficit hyperactivity disorder (ADHD), oppositional defiant disorder (OD), and conduct disorder (CD) (Loeber and Hay 1997).

Table 2.4 lists selected symptoms of the various psychiatric disorders of childhood that in long-term follow-up studies predict later delinquency. Before readers start to make self-diagnoses, recall that the duration and intensity of symptoms are part of diagnostic criteria. Just because you found a class boring and spent your time fidgeting does not mean that you should be diagnosed with attention deficit disorder. Nor does an occasional impulsive act—like a late-night raid on the refrigerator—qualify as a true symptom of the impulsivity component of hyperactivity.

Table 2.4

Examples of Symptoms of Childhood Psychiatric Disorders

Conduct Disorder Symptoms

1. Is physically cruel to animals.
2. Destroys others' property on purpose.
3. Starts physical fights with people at home.
4. Lies to get out of trouble.

Impulsivity Symptoms

1. Acts before thinking.
2. Does dangerous things without thinking; for example, runs into the street without looking.

Inattention Symptoms

1. Has a hard time planning how to do activities.
2. Makes careless mistakes in schoolwork or other activities.

Hyperactivity Symptoms

1. Runs about or climbs where or when he or she should not.
2. Appears to be "on the go" or "driven by a motor."

Source: Emory DSM Rating Scale (EDRS)—Parent Version.

The symptoms of conduct disorder do resemble—indeed, are sometimes identical to—items on a self-report delinquency questionnaire. However, this does not mean that psychiatry and criminology view delinquency in the same way. Criminologists adopt a more continuous view of individual differences; they see no sharp division between the nondelinquent, mild delinquent, and serious delinquent. In the tradition of general medicine, psychiatry tends to view disorders as categorical. One either has the flu or does not; there are no people who are one-fourth flu affected and three-fourths normal. The common symptoms of flu, such as fevers and aches, usually occur together in a syndrome. Most critically, the flu has a decisive causal etiology, a single virus that spreads easily from person to person and causes the disease; a flu vaccine can protect against this virus.

In contrast, although different ADHD and CD symptoms intercorrelate, it is unclear whether they can constitute a true syndrome. Another complexity is introduced because ADHD and CD are often co-morbid (psychiatric terminology for "co-occurrence") with anxiety and depression, making the diagnostic syndrome seem too broad in its behavioral content. You should be aware, then, that psychiatrists usually prefer to diagnose (classify) and to make comparisons between diagnosed cases and controls who do not qualify for a diagnosis. Whether the psychiatric disorders are true syndromes, with special etiology (causes) and highly structured symptoms, like many medical diseases, is debatable. I cannot resolve this issue in this text, but I admit to my bias toward treating the diagnosed cases as an extreme end of a continuum.

In adulthood, the DSM-IV can be used to make a formal diagnosis of antisocial personality disorder. This diagnosis is heavily weighted by a past history of violations of social norms and criminal acts (i.e., stealing, traffic arrests). Although not a formal diagnosis, a more interesting classification of adults is *psychopathy* as a personality disorder. Psychopathy scales contain a number of personality characteristics that are more frequent in a population of criminal offenders than in the general population (Hare 1985). These include lack of anxiety, lack of remorse or shame, selfishness, inflated self-esteem, deceit, poor judgment, impulsivity, failure to learn from experience, and a false charm and intelligence. The biological processes that differentiate psychopathic individuals from the ordinary citizen and the run-of-the mill criminal have been extensively investigated.

Although the majority of psychiatrically ill individuals are not criminal, the major psychoses of depression and schizophrenia may also contribute to crime, especially to more bizarre and rare types of crimes. The accompanying Box 2.2 describes the relationship of these psychiatric disorders to rampage killings. In this book I do not emphasize the major psychoses because, although psychotic individuals' crimes are often headline-grabbing, these disorders are rarely contributors to criminal behavior. The existence of this route into crime, however, emphasizes once again the heterogeneity of the population of criminals. To assert, as Gottfredson and Hirschi (1990) do in their general theory of crime, that only a single temperamental profile causally underlies crime (e.g., low self-control) is an oversimplification. As much as it would be convenient to have just one story of how criminals are both born or made, many subtypes of criminals actually exist. By emphasizing the most common psychiatric and temperamental profiles—e.g., the lack of guilt, low self-control, and other more common traits—we make a convenient simplification of the heterogeneity of personality dispositions underlying criminal behavior.

Box 2.2

Psychiatric Illness and Rampage Killers

Rampage killers commit apparently senseless crimes with multiple victims. Kip Kinkel, an Oregon boy, wounded 25 classmates and killed two; he also killed his parents, who had worried about Kip's fascination with violence. Psychiatric evaluation found that Kip had a hallmark symptom of schizophrenia: auditory hallucinations. One voice would call him nasty names while a second would order him to kill. Kip's family tree was also loaded with psychiatric illness, with five cousins having a psychiatric diagnosis. Paranoid schizophrenia primed Kinkel to commit these senseless acts of violence (National Desk 1999).

Thanks to an article in the *New York Times* (Fessenden 2000), we have a profile of 102 killers in 100 rampage attacks. Their attacks resulted in the deaths of 425 people and in injuries to 510 more. These killers showed symptoms of psychiatric disturbance and were unlike garden-variety street criminals. They were better educated than ordinary criminals but were less likely to be employed. My interpretation is that their psychiatric illnesses prevented them from achieving an occupational success equal to their academic potential. None of the rampage killers made an effort to avoid being caught by the police.

Of the 102 rampage killers, 48 had a formal psychiatric diagnosis; 24 were taking a prescribed psychiatric drug; and 14 had stopped their medication just before committing their crimes. It should be emphasized, especially to those readers with a psychiatric illness in a family member, that most people with a major psychosis are not violent. However, psychosis can increase the risk of violence, especially of this extreme and bizarre sort.

Finally, there is also a large research literature on the heritability of psychiatric diagnoses. An adoption study of schizophrenia conducted in the 1960s (Heston 1966) was actually one of the most influential post-World War II spurs to the field of behavioral genetics. In the 1970s, the scientific view of the causation of the major psychoses shifted from inadequate maternal parenting styles (fathers never got much blame) to biology, including genetic inheritance. A shift in thinking about ADHD, ODD, and CD, the childhood disorders with the closest links to crime, is currently underway. Large twin studies in England, America, and Australia have confirmed the genetic inheritance of ADHD (Eaves et al. 1997; Levy et al. 1997; Thapar, Hervas, and McGuffin 1995). Shared environmental influences seem minimal, however. Diagnoses of ODD and CD are also heritable. Yet in many but not all behavioral genetic studies, the diagnosis of CD was influenced by shared familial environments. This finding resonates back to the small twin studies of delinquency summarized above, in which shared environmental influences were particularly strong—e.g., the fraternal twin pairs were almost as alike in their delinquency rates as the identical twin pairs. Thus, work in psychiatry supports the idea that when ADHD and ODD children grow up, they will be genetically different from noncriminals, and also from criminals who may not have displayed these symptoms as children.

Conclusion

Criminal disposition is one of the more complex traits studied by behavioral geneticists. The source of this disposition is heterogeneous. In some cases, it lies in psychoses; more commonly, it lies in a variety of temperamental and personality traits associated with diagnoses of childhood disorders in psychiatry, or with the presence of psychopathy in adulthood. A broad range of evidence suggests that criminal disposition is heritable, including studies of psychiatric disorders, crime-linked personality traits, and crime itself, both as criminal acts recorded by the courts and police and as self-reported ones. On the other hand, crime is environmentally influenced as well. Twins, for example, can be partners in crime; they rarely jointly take an IQ test or receive a job interview simultaneously. There is also an interaction of genetic by environmental influences in the genesis of criminal disposition, as discussed further in chapter 6.

Recommended Reading

Plomin, R., J. C. DeFries, G. E. McClearn, and P. McGuffin. 2000. *Behavioral Genetics* (4th ed.). New York: Worth Publishers. This text is an excellent introduction to the field of behavioral genetics for the novice student.

References

Bohman, M., C. R. Cloninger, S. Sigvardsson, and A. L. von Knorring. 1982. "Predisposition to Petty Criminality in Swedish Adoptees: I. Genetic and Environmental Heterogeneity." *Archives of General Psychiatry* 39: 1233–1241.

Bouchard, T. Jr., D. T. Lykken, M. McGue, N. L. Segal, and A. Tellegen. 1990. "Sources of Human Psychological Differences: The Minnesota Study of Twins Reared Apart." *Science* 250: 223–228.

Cadoret, R. J., W. R. Yates, E. Troughton, G. Woodworth, and M. A. Stewart. 1995. "Genetic-environmental Interaction in the Genesis of Aggressivity and Conduct Disorders." *Archives of General Psychiatry* 52: 916–924.

Cloninger, C. R., S. Sigvardsson, M. Bohman, and A. L. von Knorring. 1982. "Predispositions to Petty Criminality in Swedish Adoptees: II. Cross-fostering Analysis of Gene-environment Interactions." *Archives of General Psychiatry* 39: 1242–1247.

Corballis, M. C. 1997. "The Genetics and Evolution of Handedness." *Psychological Review* 104: 714–727.

DiLalla, L. F. and I. I. Gottesman. 1990. "Heterogeneity of Causes for Delinquency and Criminality: Lifespan Perspectives." *Development and Psychopathology* 1: 339–349.

Eaves, L. J., J. L. Silberg, J. M. Meyer, H. H. Maes, E. Simonoff, A. Pickles, M. Rutter, M. C. Neale, C. A. Reynolds, M. T. Erickson, A. C. Heath, R. Loeber, K. R. Truett, and J. K. Hewitt. 1997. "Genetics and Developmental Psychopathology: 2. The Main Effects of Genes and Environment on Behavioral Problems in the Virginia Study of Adolescent Behavioral Development." *Journal of Child Psychology and Psychiatry* 38: 965–980.

Faraone, S. V., M. T. Tsuang, and D. W. Tsuang. 1999. *Genetics of Mental Disorders: A Guide for Students, Clinicians, and Researchers.* New York: Guilford Press.

Fessenden, F. 2000. "They Threaten, Seethe and Unhinge, Then Kill in Quantity." *New York Times,* 9 April 2000, 28–29.

Gold, M. (1970). *Delinquent Behavior in an American City.* Belmont, CA: Brooks-Cole.

Gottesman, I. I. 1991. *Schizophrenia Genesis: The Origins of Madness.* New York: W. H. Freeman.

Gottfredson, M. R. and T. Hirschi, 1990. *A General Theory of Crime*. Stanford, CA: Stanford University Press.

Grove, W. M., E. D. Eckert, L. Heston, T. J. Bouchard, Jr., N. Segal, and D. T. Lykken. 1990. "Heritability of Substance Abuse and Antisocial Behavior: A Study of Monozygotic Twins Reared Apart." *Biological Psychiatry* 27: 1293–1304.

Hare, R. D. 1985. "Comparison of Procedures for the Assessment of Psychopathy." *Journal of Consulting and Clinical Psychology* 53: 7 16.

Harris, J. R. 1995. "Where Is the Child's Environment? A Group Socialization Theory of Development." *Psychological Review* 102: 458–489.

Heston, L. L. 1966. "Psychiatric Disorders in Foster Home Reared Children of Schizophrenic Mothers." *British Journal of Psychiatry* 112: 819–825.

Kanazawa, S. and M. C. Still. 2000. "Why Men Commit Crimes (and Why They Desist)." *Sociological Theory* 18: 434–447.

Laland, K. N., J. Kumm, J. D. Van Horn, and M. W. Feldman. 1995. "A Gene-culture Model of Human Handedness." *Behavior Genetics* 25: 433–445.

Levy, F., D. A. Hay, M. McStephen, C. Wood, and I. Waldman. 1997. "Attention-deficit Hyperactivity Disorder: A Category or a Continuum? Genetic Analysis of a Large Scale Twin Study." *Journal of the American Academy of Child and Adolescent Psychiatry* 36: 737–744.

Loeber, R., S. M. Green, B. B. Lahey, P. J. Frick, and K. McBurnett. 2000. "Findings on Disruptive Behavior Disorders From the First Decade of the Developmental Trends Study." *Clinical Child and Family Psychology Review* 3: 37–60.

Loeber, R. and D. Hay. 1997. "Key Issues in the Development of Aggression and Violence From Childhood to Early Adulthood." *Annual Review of Psychology* 48: 371–410.

Loehlin, J. C. 1992. *Genes and Environment in Personality Development*. Newbury Park, CA: Sage Publications.

—. 1993. "Nature, Nurture, and Conservatism in the Australian Twin Study." *Behavior Genetics* 23: 287–290.

Loehlin, J. C. and R. C. Nichols. 1976. *Heredity, Environment, and Personality*. Austin, TX: University of Texas Press.

Lombroso, G. and C. Lombroso. 1972. *Criminal Man, According to the Classification of Cesare Lombroso*. Montclair, NJ: Patterson Smith.

McCartney, K., and R. Rosenthal. 2000. "Effect Size, Practical Importance, and Social Policy for Children." *Child Development* 71: 173–180.

Mednick, S. A. 2000. Personal communication (October).

Mednick, S. A., W. F. Gabrielli, Jr., and H. Hutchings. 1984. "Genetic Influences in Criminal Convictions: Evidence From an Adoption Cohort." *Science* 224: 891–894.

Miles, D. R. and G. Carey. 1997. "Genetic and Environmental Architecture of Human Aggression." *Journal of Personality and Social Psychology* 72: 207–217.

Moffitt, T. E. 1993. "Adolescence-limited and Life-course Persistent Antisocial Behavior: A Developmental Taxonomy." *Psychological Review* 100: 674–701.

Nagin, D. and R. E. Tremblay. 1999. "Trajectories of Boys' Physical Aggression, Opposition, and Hyperactivity on the Path to Physically Violent and Nonviolent Juvenile Delinquency." *Child Development* 70: 1181–1196.

National Desk. 1999. "Live in Fear, Oregon School Killer Is Told." 6 November 1999, A11.

Rowe, D. C. 1983. "Biometrical Genetic Models of Self-reported Delinquent Behavior: A Twin Study." *Behavior Genetics* 13: 473–489.

—. 1994. *The Limits of Family Influence: Genes, Experience, and Behavior.* New York: Guilford Press.

Rowe, D. C., D. M. Almeida, and K. C. Jacobson. 1999. "Genetic and School Context Influences on Aggression in Adolescence." *Psychological Science* 10: 277–280.

Segal, N. 1999. *Entwined Lives: Twins and What They Tell Us About Human Behavior.* New York: Patton.

Stryker, J. 1997. "Twin Pique: Yin, Yang, and You." *New York Times*, 7 September 1997, 4E.

Stunkard, A. J., T. I. A. Sorensen, C. Hanis, T. W. Teasdale, R. Chakraborty, W. J. Schull, and F. Schulsinger. 1986. "An Adoption Study of Human Obesity." *New England Journal of Medicine* 314: 193–198.

Thapar, A., A. Hervas, and P. McGuffin. 1995. "Childhood Hyperactivity Scores Are Highly Heritable and Show Sibling Competition Effects: Twin Study Evidence." *Behavior Genetics* 25: 537–544.

Tremblay, R. E., C. Japel, D. Perusse, P. McDuff, M. Boivin, M. Zoccolillo, and J. Montplaisir. 1999. "The Search for the Age of 'Onset' of Physical Aggression: Rousseau and Bandura Revisited. *Criminal Behavior and Mental Health* 9: 8–23. ✦

Chapter 3

The Evolutionary Perspective on Crime

For every one female killer, about nine men are murderers. For every one woman who kills another unrelated woman, about 30 men kill an unrelated man (Daly and Wilson 1988). The gender imbalance in the killing of same-sex acquaintances or strangers is one of the most extreme behavioral differences known between the sexes.

Criminologists sometimes quip that a gene for crime exists, and it is on the Y chromosome. One X chromosome and one Y chromosome make a person male; two X chromosomes, a female. The Y chromosome is the carrier of maleness, which is now known to be determined by the SRY gene. Unlike the real SRY gene, some other "genes" humorously attributed to the Y chromosome include those for TV channel flipping, not listening, and spitting in the street. Seriously, though, the gender difference in crime rates, especially in violent crime, demands a scientific explanation.

One explanation of gender differences focuses on how boys and girls are socialized in different ways. Young boys and girls certainly behave differently. The most obvious gender differences are in toy choices: Boys prefer to play with trucks and guns; girls prefer to play with dolls and kitchen sets. Parents can be upset when children choose gender-inappropriate toys. One theory about this gender difference is that it is produced by differences in the ways in which girls and boys are treated by their parents, who in turn embody the values and attitudes of a broader culture.

A possible problem with this cultural explanation is that boys and girls may innately prefer these gender-typed toys and that our materialistic society works overtime to satisfy their desires. A toy company could immediately double its sales if it could produce a toy—a hybrid between Barbie and a G.I. Joe?—that sold well to both genders. An economic incentive exists for such a toy, but so far toy companies have been unsuccessful in perfecting a toy with "dual-sex appeal." In some girls, a genetic hormone disorder exposes their brain to a variant of testosterone, the big *T* of masculinity. Not only do these girls prefer to play with male gender-typed toys, they insist that their parents buy the toys for them (Berenbaum and Hines 1992; Berenbaum, personal communication). So it may be that culture is simply responding to children's prior preferences.

Cultural explanations can also get stuck in a kind of circular reasoning. If in this generation we socialize each gender to prefer just the gender-typed toys, why did we decide to socialize them in this way and when? If these socialization practices existed four generations ago, were they started five generations ago? A Hindu sage was once asked what holds up the earth. He replied, "A turtle." The questioner persisted, "What holds the turtle up?" The sage shook his head and responded, "It's turtles all the way down." So, too, is the source of sex differences "cultural" all the way down? It is, unless we can get a grasp at what motivates a culture to socialize in a particular way and what maintains its practices of inculcating the young over generations.

Perspectives on Human Behavior and Evolution

Evolutionary perspectives on human behavior reach into the distant past and extend to before written records, when *Homo sapiens* were not the only humanlike species roaming the earth. According to a theory of human origins based on the molecular clock of human mitochondrial DNA, modern humans first originated in Africa (Ingman et al. 2000). These first humans left Africa about 100,000 years ago and moved first into Asia. The Asian migration branch reached all the way to Australia some 40,000 to 60,000 years ago and settled in North America a relatively recent 20,000 years ago. People from Africa arrived in Europe about 40,000 years ago and probably replaced another humanlike species, the Neanderthals. This prehistorical epoch, the Pleistocene, extending from some 1.6 million years ago until about 10,000 years ago—that is, from after the human line's separation from a common ancestor with the chimpanzee through the Ice Ages, but before the beginning of written history—is a period in which the *Homo sapiens'* brain and behavior were evolutionarily shaped.

There is no single evolutionarily based theory of human behavior. E. O. Wilson first proposed sociobiology in a broadly synthetic work published in 1975. The first 26 chapters dealt with animal behavior; only the last chapter covered how evolution may have shaped human behavior. Wilson earned the enmity of many social scientists, however, when he wrote that neurobiology and evolutionary theory would yield "an enduring set of first principles" for disciplines such as sociology (575). Sociobiology focuses on the evolutionary roots of social behaviors such as parental care and solicitude, aggression, the preference for herds or for a solitary existence, and altruism. In 1992, Tooby and Cosmides proposed another variant of applying evolution to human behavior and called the field evolutionary psychology. This field emphasizes dispositions in the mind—mental modules, as they are called—over overt behavior (Crawford and Krebs 1998). Despite some differences in their details, evolutionary approaches share some broad basic principles. These principles can help you to understand how evolutionary theorists think about behavior and how their analysis can then be applied to the origins of criminal behavior.

Design and Adaptation

A core assumption of the evolutionary approach is that the brain is adapted to make particular behavioral choices, with each choice solving an adaptive problem during the course of human evolution. Such adaptations are seen as designs because they are finely worked to respond to particular environmental pressures with particular behavioral solutions. For example, people the world over must find a mate with whom to have their children. One adaptive problem is attracting the attention of the opposite sex.

Young people today do so with methods that certainly did not exist in the Pleistocene, such as having cars with overpowered stereo speakers. On the other hand, some aspects of attracting the opposite sex are inborn and universal. Women's facial expressions during flirting—smiling, raising eyebrows, and casting away the eyes—are found the world over. The ethologist Eibl-Eibesfeldt (1970) demonstrated this fact with a clever apparatus: a camera with hidden sideways lens that photographed people standing near him while it appeared he was photographing a distant landscape. In general, a number of aspects of facial expression show universality across human cultures (Ekman 1994).

The ability of evolution to create complex designs, both in the physical body and in the brain, is a marvel to behold. A full discussion of the mechanism of evolution requires a book; I encourage you to pick up Richard Dawkins' (1987) *The Blind Watchmaker* to learn more. But to give a simple description, I can note that evolution works in two steps. In the first step, random genetic mutation of DNA creates variants of physical and mental characteristics. Most of these mutational changes are harmful: The offspring die in utero or shortly after birth, or, if they do reach adulthood, they have fewer progeny than other individuals in the population. Occasionally, a mutation is advantageous. Bearers of the mutation survive better and longer and thus have more offspring than others in the population; as a result, this mutational change spreads. This second step is called *selection*; it preserves the DNA changes that are beneficial to individuals and eliminates those that are harmful. Because evolution combines these two steps, random mutation and selection, complex and highly improbable structures can be built slowly over time.

As an analogy, consider a situation in which Joe flips 20 of Oscar's quarters. Oscar tells Joe he can keep all the quarters that turn up heads. The chance is only .00000095 that Joe will gain all 20 quarters. Now suppose a rule like that of natural selection is operating. Each "head" on the coin is like a favorable genetic change. Joe is allowed to keep a quarter when it comes up heads, and he now only flips those quarters that come up tails. In a short time, Joe will have five dollars in his pocket, all because he collects the quarters as they turn up heads; in this way, the improbable becomes very possible under an evolutionary process.

Sexual Selection

Darwin's phrase "the struggle for existence" conjures up images of men fighting lions or of families braving a winter blizzard. Natural selection is most often thought of as people having to survive against the forces of nature: the physical environment and other species. Darwin, however, saw another selective force, one much closer to home:

the competition within a species for opportunities to mate and to raise offspring to adulthood. Darwin observed that the iridescent tail feathers on a male peacock are an impractical trait. Heavy to haul around, they may slow flight away from a predator that views the peacock as a quick meal. So why grow ostentatious feathers? For only one reason: to woo the female. The peacock that mates successfully contributes genes to the next generation; his tail-feather poor "peers" die without mating and passing on their genes.

As Darwin and contemporary evolutionary theorists have observed, sexual selection is inherently an unequal process because of the different roles the two sexes play in bearing offspring. In mammals, females carry their fetus during pregnancy and nourish their offspring with breast milk after birth. Males of many mammalian species provide little more than sperm as their contribution to the start of the next generation. The less males contribute to the protection and provisioning of the young, the more they are free to compete with other males for access to females. Conversely, the more females invest in maternal care toward their young, the more costly it becomes for them to compete intensely with other females for mates. An important prediction of sexual selection theory is that when females provide little parental care and solicitude toward their own offspring, as is the case in some bird species, they will behave more like male mammals in the arena of sexual competition; this prediction has been upheld (Alcock 1997).

Forms of sexual selection vary greatly among species, with not all forms echoing the poet Tennyson's "nature red in tooth and claw." In the prairie grouse, the adult males parade around the lek (an area where birds sexually display), strutting their great masculinity, while the females pick and choose. In one species of ground squirrel, males rush from female to female and "politely" line up waiting their turn. If the line for a female is too long, the male runs to another burrow hoping to find a more available female. The male bowerbird of New Guinea decorates its bower—a large structure built on the ground—with bright objects, including human-manufactured ones, to attract a female.

Despite these nonviolent forms of sexual competition, sexual selection may produce a more violent form of male-male confrontation. In a recent news report, a man was attacked by a male deer with a rack of antlers; the fellow held onto the antlers and managed to kill the enraged deer with his pocketknife, lucky to come away with just bad bruises. Such antlers grow only on the male deer and only in rutting (mating) season, when the males go at each other violently to earn the opportunity to inseminate the does. Why the buck decided to attack a man instead of another deer is unknown, but bucks not only become better armored in rutting season, they exhibit a more aggressive temperament.

In summary, sexual selection is the evolutionary process responsible for sexual dimorphisms—sex differences in physical traits and in the instinctive drives that put those physical differences to work.

Kin Selection

Family gatherings are such an everyday part of life that they are unremarkable. Kin show caring and love for one another, and the attachment between parent and child is one of the strongest human bonds. Kin selection explains the evolution of altruism, including love, affection, and caring toward biological relatives. In evolutionary theory, *altruism* has the special meaning of doing something for a biological relative today that may reduce the altruist's future reproductive success. The paradox of altruism is most clearly seen in social insects, such as some species of ants, in which workers will sacrifice their own lives for the good of a colony.

Kin selection occurs because relatives share alleles (gene variants) according to the coefficient of genetic relatedness. A gene that exists in a parent's body has a 50 percent chance of existing in his or her child's body. A gene that exists in a sister's body has 50 percent chance of also being in her brother's body. Thus, genes can still propagate from one generation to the next when an altruistic act correspondingly increases the reproductive success of a biological relative who received the benefits of the altruism. To equate the loss of genes from a relative's death, more relatives must be saved than the reciprocal of the coefficient of genetic relatedness (e.g., $1/\frac{1}{2} = 2$). A father can thus give his life for more than two children, a brother for more than two siblings, and a cousin for more than eight cousins. I don't really believe, though, that a father or mother makes such a calculation when saving a single child from a burning home. It is the principle that matters: Small acts of altruism that confer reproductive benefits to kin at small costs to the altruist are evolutionarily favored.

Life History Traits

Evolutionary theory also makes predictions about life history traits—those traits determinative of survival and reproduction. Among important life history traits are the timing of pubertal development, of the age to bear children, and of birth spacing and the decision to bear fewer children and invest much effort in their upbringing or more children and invest less effort in each. Across species, two extreme life course histories are distinguished: *r-selected species,* which are opportunistic, have many offspring, reproduce quickly, and have short life spans, and *K-selected species,* such as humans, which have the opposite suite of life history traits, such as long gestation time during pregnancy, slow development, few and widely spaced births, and long life spans. Species that are *r* selected are well adapted to colonizing environments with little competition from conspecifics (i.e., other members of their own species). The letter *r* stands for "population growth rate" in a demographic equation that predicts population growth. Various types of ecological pressures can favor a species evolving towards either an *r* or a *K* organization of life history traits. For example, highly variable environments may favor *r* type characteristics because a rapidly reproducing organism can best take advantage of a rapid shift from inadequate food supplies to abundant ones.

Sexual Selection and Sex Differences in Crime

This chapter opened with the puzzle of the large gender difference in crime. Rates of nearly all types of crimes, and especially more serious ones such as robbery and murder, are greater for males than for females. If this finding were true just in the United States, the explanation could focus on something peculiar about our culture that makes men violent. However, the greater crime rates of males occurs in all cultures and, notwithstanding stories of Amazon women, throughout the historical record as well.

The sexual selection explanation is that men's bodies and brains are adapted for greater use of threat and violence against others (Daly and Wilson 1988). On average, men are taller and stronger than women. If men and women are paired at random, nine times out of 10 the man will be the taller of the pair. Men's upper-body strength is about double that of women, even adjusting for body size differences. To the evolutionist, these physical-trait differences are proof of past sexual selection in which men competed for access to females more than the converse, women competing for access to males. These well-known physical differences between the genders are disregarded by all sociological theories of crime, yet their existence is central in an evolutionary account of gender differences.

To account for these differences in physical characteristics and behavior, we must suppose that those males who used aggressive tactics in the Pleistocene had greater reproductive success than nonaggressive males did—that is, more surviving children. In this case, evolution would favor genes that promoted risk taking and aggression in males. (See Box 3.1 for details on how a slight reproductive advantage could favor the intensification of male aggression over generations.) Not that the use of aggression to deter rivals and control women ended in the Pleistocene. In a Bill Moyers TV special, an inner-city boy was asked about his violent acts. He said that a guy had messed with his girl, so he hammered nails into a board and hit his rival with it.

Without condoning this brutish behavior, it can be observed that delinquent youths are not "maladapted" from a Darwinian perspective. In the Cambridge Study in Delinquent Development, the number of children born to parents with criminal convictions was actually greater than the number born to the remaining parents (N = 3.91 children versus 3.12 children, *p* .0001; Lynn 1995). In the United States, inner-city fathers were more than twice as likely to be delinquent as inner-city nonfathers (Stouthamer-Loeber and Wei 1998).

We do not know, of course, whether this advantage has existed in every generation, extending back thousands of years. However, it must have existed frequently enough to produce the visible sexual dimorphism between men and women. It is noteworthy that the reproductive success of delinquent and criminal individuals is in sharp contrast to the reduced reproductive success of individuals given a diagnosis of a major psychosis. For example, schizophrenic men and women are, on average, much less likely to marry and have offspring than people without a mental illness (Gottesman 1991, 196), and their schizophrenia-predisposing genes would be expected to disappear from a population over many generations. Why they have not done so is a major scientific mystery.

Our focus on the more violence-prone male does not imply that women refrain from competing with one another. Studies of aggression have taken to considering backbiting and gossip among women

Box 3.1

How Male Aggression Could Intensify Over Generations

Suppose that at birth a population is 30 percent aggressive males and 70 percent nonaggressive males. In this simplified case, the aggressive males carry a dominant gene that enhances the tendency to be aggressive. Whether that gene will spread in later generations will depend on the average number of surviving children among the 30 percent aggressive males versus the 70 percent nonaggressive ones. Suppose that 5 percent of the aggressive males actually die before they reach reproductive age. In the population of reproductive-age males, .26 are aggressive [.26 = .25/(.25+.70)] and .74 [.70/(.25+.70)] are nonaggressive. The early death of aggressive men has tipped the population composition further in favor of nonaggressive men. However, suppose that each of the surviving aggressive males had nine children and the nonaggressive males had on average three children. The aggressive males could achieve their greater reproductive success through possessing several mates. In the anthropological record, cultures with polygyny—one man with several wives—as the legal or legitimate form of marital union have greatly outnumbered those permitting only monogamous forms of marriage. In such cases, the average number of children is greater per aggressive man than per his nonaggressive rival:

(1) Children per aggressive man = .26 x 9 = 2.34

(2) Children per nonaggressive man = .74 x 3 = 2.22

Two conclusions can be drawn from the numbers in this hypothetical example. The first is that the population has the potential to grow in size because more than two children are born per couple. The second conclusion is that the gene predisposing toward aggression will become more common because the 2.34 children born to aggressive men exceeds the 2.22 born to nonaggressive men. Although in one generation, this effect may seem small (.12 children per generation), over many generations its cumulative impact on gene frequencies may be large. Nonetheless, it is unlikely that population would grow to include only aggressive men, because intermale aggression carries many social costs. At some point the process would probably stabilize, a form of natural selection called *frequency dependent selection.*

The main point is that when risky, dangerous tactics yield large reproductive payoffs, they are likely to be favored by sexual selection. And that is especially so for males than for females, because a single male can amplify his reproductive success through having multiple wives, whereas women cannot accomplish the same reproductive increases by having multiple husbands.

as forms of aggression. Such communications can inflict damage on the reputation and status of rivals for a woman's romantic partner, just as direct physical aggression can be used by males to discourage their romantic rivals. Thus, the characterization of these female behaviors as a form of aggression is probably correct. They also serve to illustrate, however, the implication of evolutionary theory that in competition with romantic rivals, women would be less likely to adopt forms of aggression that lead to injury or death.

According to sexual selection theory, males would be more willing to use violence than females in situations of sexual rivalry. And some crimes do fall directly into this category, when they result from men being in conflict over a woman or from an act of violence provoked by the danger of a loss of status to a man, which could indirectly worsen his chances with romantically interested women. When I taught at the University of Oklahoma in the 1980s, one football player shot another in the athletic dorm. According to press reports, the shooter was a running back who had been humiliated in front of his friends by a large lineman. When the shooter returned with a small handgun, the big guy taunted him to shoot, which he did. Fortunately, the bullet passed through the big football player without causing serious injury. These former acquaintances saw an altercation escalate out of control, but in evolutionary terms, preserving one's reputation can be worth the risk inherent in horrible acts of violence.

Other crimes, like robbery, do not seem directly linked to sexual rivalry. Violence in a robbery is sometimes unintended—a victim resists giving up his or her property, and the robber stabs or shoots the victim. One way to connect these crimes with evolutionary advantage is that they enable men to amass the property needed to attract women faster than they could through honest work. Of course, this logic presumes that women would be sexually attracted to someone who is criminal. Certainly Hollywood movies make this a staple theme, but movie criminals who catch the leading lady are always good at heart behind their rough exteriors, and they are more handsome than just about anyone. For an evolutionary theorist, one must ask, what is the evolutionary advantage for women to be attracted to men who steal and threaten others, if such men may be ostracized by the community?

Gangestad and Simpson (1990) have proposed one possible answer to this question: the *sexy son hypothesis.* According to this hypothesis, women are sexually attracted to men who may be poor providers as husbands but who are handsome, muscular, and socially dominant–traits that a criminal as well as a sports hero can possess. What women want, not necessarily in any conscious sense, are the "good" genes that these men provide, because their sons will possess half of their father's genes and will possibly be, just as their fathers were, magnets for female affection with correspondingly greater opportunities for their own reproductive success. The same "mental module" could account for female groupies that surround rock stars, sports heroes, and even famous politicians (as in the phrase, "power is the best aphrodisiac"). In sum, sexual selection can give a broad-brush explanation for why men are more physically aggressive and risk taking than females, traits that characterize both criminals and adventurers. At the same time, this evolutionary explanation requires both a male and female perspective. The theory is both more complex, and more indeterminate, than this short presentation can do full justice to.

Life History, Sexual Selection, and the Age-Crime Curve

People intuitively recognize that males' potential danger to them varies by age. Adults are more likely to move away from a group of three or four teenage boys than away from a golfing foursome of older men. Not that the criminal urge dissipates entirely with age. I was once amused watching, but not feeling threatened by, some older motorcyclists sporting an array of tattoos. One of them suddenly and maliciously took his cigarette and popped several advertising balloons–a little of the old antisocial juices still flowed.

In an article that attracted considerable attention among criminologists, Gottfredson and Hirschi (1983) proposed the existence of a universal relationship between age and crime. According to their summary of the world's data, across many historical periods and in many societies, property and violent crime appeared to peak in the late teenage years. Before this peak, there was an accelerated rise in the crime rate. That is, from 10 to about 17 years of age the proportion of all youths who committed crimes increased. After that peak, the crime rate fell off rapidly in the early 20s. Individuals in the population thus seem to be quitting their criminal activities at this time. A crime rate may also increase because the same people commit more crimes per year. However, most of the change in crime rates appears to involve the addition of adolescents who had not committed a crime before. Individual crime rates do not change as much, partly because criminals do not spend most of their time committing crimes (e.g., they are watching TV, eating, sleeping, shopping for groceries, and doing the things we all do). Not every crime conforms perfectly to the age-crime curve (Steffensmeier et al. 1989); for instance, gambling peaks later than in adolescence; it is somewhat like drug addiction in this regard. Yet despite these caveats, the age-crime curve is robust enough to require an explanation.

In my adaptive strategy theory of crime (Rowe 1996), I propose an explanation in terms of the life history of mating effort and parenting effort. Mating effort refers to the time and energy spent finding a mate and protecting him or her from rivals. Parenting effort refers to the care invested in rearing young, including pregnancy and lactation, protecting against predators (which in our species are usually microbes instead of large mammals), and transferring to offspring the skills and knowledge needed for survival as an adult.

For males, mating effort also involves a competition for access to females, as described in the section on sexual selection. Clearly, in adolescence mating effort is a priority because puberty makes an adolescent boy both interested in sex and capable of reproduction and because young boys, for the most part, have no sexual partners and have not fathered a child. Thus, their first priority is mating effort, with its attendant risks from the mild (a girl turns down a request for a date) to the major (a flirtation leads to a physical attack from the girl's boyfriend). The teenage boy needs to quickly establish his reputation and to acquire the material things that make him attractive to the opposite sex, which can be anything from a surfboard to a low-rider car.

The costs and benefits shift, however, as a young man successfully acquires a romantic partner or spouse. Because he has a mate, he no longer needs to compete against other young and older men for mating opportunities. Once a baby is born, his choices become more stark. Parenting efforts can increase, helping ensure that his child survives and prospers. (Even in the much disparaged "inner city" of U.S. cities, many young men provide some kind of economic support or attentiveness to their illegitimate children.) In contrast, continued mating effort may expose him to a variety of risks that endanger his child's health and psychological growth. For example, Billy can spend his evenings at the local bar with his buddies and risk getting into a bar fight or inciting his wife's jealousy, or he can stay at home with his wife and their one-year-old son. In the long run, the latter choice is usually the better one for the child's physical and psychological health.

Advancing a theory of the age-crime curve using the same evolutionary principles as mine, Kanazawa and Still (2000) drew three hypothetical curves to represent age-related changes in the costs and benefits of mating effort competition. In Figure 3.1(a), the benefits of mating effort competition start at near zero prior to puberty and then rise rapidly as males attain maturity and become reproductively capable. As their ability to reproduce remains little diminished over a long period of the life course, the benefit curve remains high. In Figure 3.1(b), the costs of mating effort competition rise as males get older, increasing especially dramatically after the birth of a first child. As Kanazawa and Still wrote, at this point " . . . males' energies and resources are put to better use by protecting and investing in their existing children" (442). In other words, the men would be switching from mating effort to parenting effort, particularly in a society that does not legally permit a man to marry more than one woman at a time. Benefits minus costs yield an observed competition curve that is identical to the age-crime curve, as shown by the dark line in Figure 3.1(c). Crime peaks when the benefits of mating effort competition are highest relative to its costs. Crime rates diminish as those costs increase. According to studies cited by Kanazawa and Still (2000), marriage may reduce men's testosterone levels and thus may be one biological foundation for a reduction in mating effort after marriage. None of these cost-benefit calculations need be made at the conscious level; rather, they may arise from emotional reactions to situations that have deep evolutionary roots. It's the young men who wander, the dads who want to stay at home.

Kin Selection and Crime

The altruistic and benevolent motivations felt toward kin should inhibit crime against close relatives. Notwithstanding the bickering and sibling rivalry within families, really serious crimes should be more rare against kin than nonkin. Rates of violence against kin must be judged on the basis of opportunity; people spend a lot of time around kin, so there are greater opportunities for violence against them. Yet acts of violence against brothers or sisters, or parents, are

Figure 3.1
The Benefits and Costs of Mating Competition and the Age Crime Curve

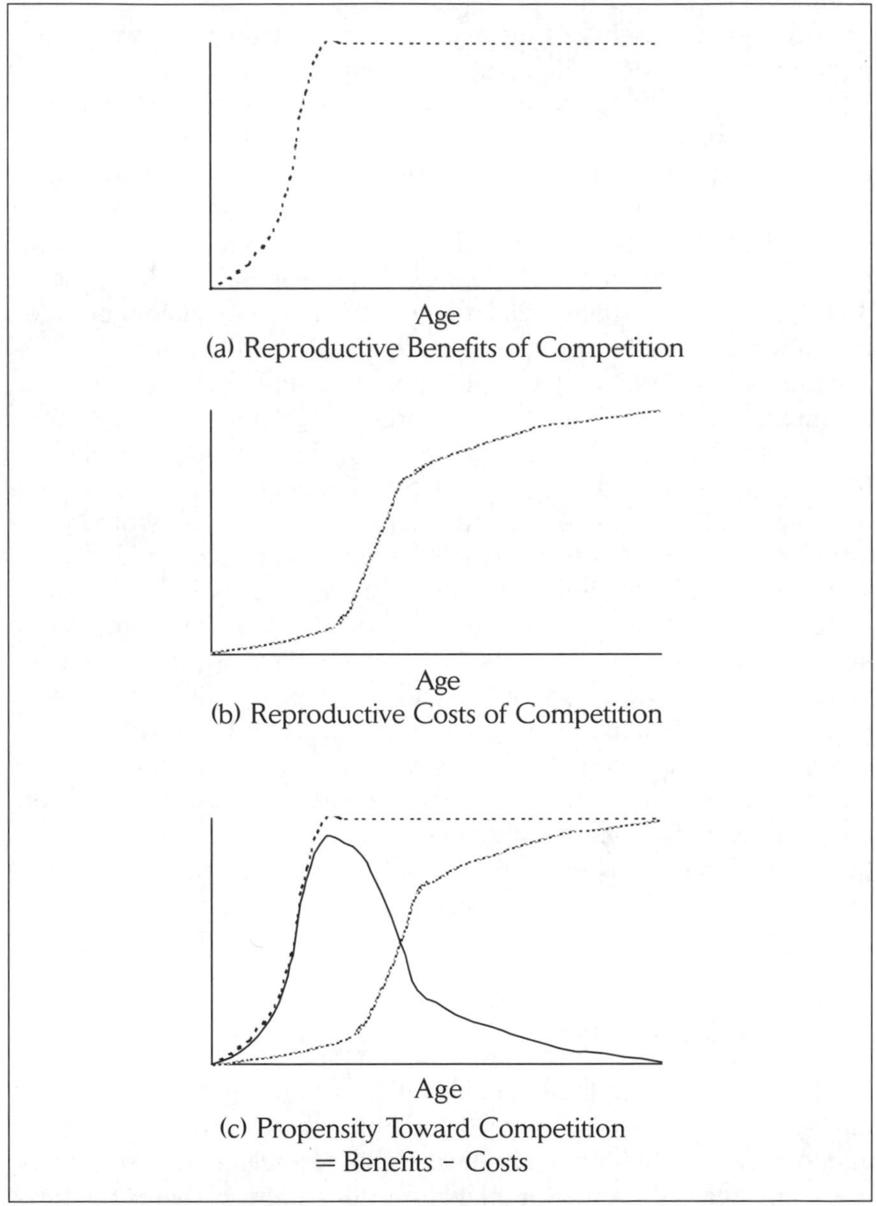

Source: Reprinted from Kanazawa, S. and M. C. Still. 2000. "Why Men Commit Crimes (and Why They Desist)." *Sociological Theory* 18, 434–447. Copyright © American Sociological Association. Reprinted by permission.

rare. On occasions when such violence does occur, it often involves a perpetrator who is psychiatrically disturbed (see Box 2.2, "Psychiatric Illness and Rampage Killers," in chapter 2).

Daly and Wilson (1988, 89) found one type of crime with which to test theories about altruism toward close kin: child abuse. A recurring theme in fairy tales is the evil stepmother. Hansel and Gretel were forced to flee into a forest because of an abusive stepmother; the beautiful Cinderella was made to labor and hide her physical appearance by her evil stepmother. And, of course, the evil queen who tried to kill Snow White was her stepmom. Moving away from folk stories to statistical evidence, Daly and Wilson examined the rate of fatal child abuse by stepparents versus biological parents. Stepparents come late to the family and share no genetic relatedness to a stepchild. The rate of fatal child abuse against a young stepchild by a stepparent was 40 to 100 times greater than that against a biological child by a biological parent. Thus, children experienced more risk of harm from biologically unrelated kin than biologically related kin. The depressing statistic on stepparents' fatal child abuse should not be misinterpreted to mean that most stepchildren have to fear their stepparents. Because serious child abuse is a rare phenomenon, most stepchildren are not abused, and most stepparents make excellent parents.

Kin altruism affects crime in another way: through co-offending (Daly and Wilson 1988; Reiss and Farrington 1991). Most criminal acts occur in small groups. Organized crime is family based, involving brothers, uncles, and nephews. Crime families adopt the language of family even when they recruit outsiders into their criminal enterprises—the criminal organization is to be family to the recruit, and blood-loyalty oaths are required. Co-offending among brothers is also common among ordinary criminals. Reiss and Farrington examined co-offending in the population-based Cambridge Study in Delinquent Development, a longitudinal study of crime conducted in England. From ages 10 to 32, according to criminal records, about half of offenses were committed alone and half with a co-offender, with solo offenses increasing as offenders got older. The most common co-offenders were unrelated males close in age to the offender. Co-offending with brothers was also fairly common, however. Seventeen percent of brothers less than two years different in age from an offender co-offended. Brothers, because they share genes, are more likely to share biological disposition towards crime than randomly paired boys or men. Because they are kin, brothers are also altruistically inclined to help one another in the commission of antisocial behaviors, which usually involves some risk. Reiss and Farrington concluded that for a choice of co-offender, ". . . there is a selection bias towards brothers" (387).

Individual Differences and Evolution

The evolutionary theory of gender differences and preference for kin is best suited to explaining how all people, or at least all of a single gender, are alike. In this way, evolutionary theory of human behavior is distinct from behavioral genetics, as the latter field explains individual differences in behavior. That is, adaptations can arise from the genes that everyone in a population shares, a type of genetic effect ignored in behavioral genetics. For example, nearly all people have four fingers and a thumb, and the genes that produce a four-fingered hand with an opposable thumb are "fixed" in the human population. *Fixed* means that every person carries two copies of the relevant genes, and the copies are identical in all persons (with perhaps minor exceptions that do not detract from the force of this example). Thus, the genes that make males more aggressive, such as ones that modulate response to and production of male sex hormones, could be fixed in all males. Such genes, and their effects, would explain the greater aggressiveness of males than females, but not how one male is more aggressive than another.

Criminal behavior, though, shows tremendous individual differences. An oft-quoted statistic in criminology is that about 5 percent of men account for 50 percent or more of all crimes committed. Whatever the exact figure, all studies find that a small minority of people commit the majority of criminal acts, especially serious ones. In self-report data on crime, a lump of people exist who report *zero* delinquent acts, whereas others report large numbers of acts. How can an evolutionary perspective explain this huge range of individual differences?

There are two possible routes of explanation. One is *conditional adaptation*. Conditional adaptations are brain mechanisms designed by evolution to react differently in response to different stimuli. Consider the body's responses to heat and cold. Heat triggers a sweating response that cools the body; cold triggers a shivering response that warms the body. These responses are adaptive mechanisms designed to protect the body against extremes of temperature. When a person is seen sweating, we do not conclude that this person possesses different genes from someone who is seen shivering; instead, we infer that the environmental trigger (temperature) was either cold or hot.

A behavioral example would be sexual jealousy (Buss 1995, 2000). People may possess an adaptive response of experiencing jealousy when they discover that a sexual partner is cheating. That is, in most people, detecting a cheating spouse or lover would instigate the jealousy "mental module." In the absence of such a trigger, jealousy would not be experienced.

The second possibility is *alternative adaptation.* In an alternative adaptation, genes are different in people who display different characteristics. Consider the heritable characteristic of lactose intolerance. Lactose is a sugar in milk that, if undigested by the enzyme lactase, causes illness. About 9,000 years ago, a change (mutation) in the lactase gene arose in Europe that gives adults an ability to digest the lactose in milk. This gene was beneficial to the European groups that herded cows and drank fresh milk, and it became more common in these populations over generations. Thus, lactose tolerant and lactose intolerant people now possess different genotypes because of the adaptive value of a change in the lactase gene (Hollox et al. 2001). As an aside, lactose tolerance is rare in African and Asian heritage people, creating a scientific debate about whether dairy products should be considered an essential food group. Lactose intolerance can be treated with a pill that assists in digesting dairy products, mimicking the effect of lactase.

Technically, an alternative adaptation requires that genetic variants be adaptive—that is, advantageous to reproductive success. There is no definitive example of an alternative adaptation in a behavioral trait in humans because it is so difficult to prove that genetic variability is adaptive in a biological sense. Genetic variation also arises that is not adaptive—for example, from the accumulation of mildly deleterious mutations that can make a nonadaptive characteristic heritable. Whatever the source of the genetic variation, heritable characteristics have a different mechanism in the behavioral response than conditional adaptations. In the former, genetic differences exist among people; in the latter, no genetic differences are present among people but different responses to environmental triggers exist.

Evolutionary Theory of Biological Differences in Criminal Disposition

A conditional adaptation theory that can be used to explain crime has been advanced by Belsky, Steinberg, and Draper (1991a) and Draper and Harpending (1982), among others. This theory places a tremendous emphasis on the early experiences of the child. According to this theory, infants and preschoolers attend to family cues and signs of either a future stable and secure environment or a future unstable and insecure environment. These cues include father absence (emphasized in Draper and Harpending's version of the theory) and inconsistent and harsh parenting styles (as emphasized more by Belsky, Steinberg, and Draper). In infancy, these cues influence the degree of attachment between infants and their mothers. Infants detecting signs of a future insecure environment tend to be insecurely attached to their mothers, whereas those detecting a more positive future tend to be securely attached.

The infants in these different groups tend to follow different life histories. The theory makes the novel prediction that insecurely attached infants will, in their late childhood or early teenage years, reach pubertal maturity before securely attached infants do. The theory also predicts more "criminal" characteristics for the insecurely attached infants when they grow up. For boys, the expected life course includes greater aggression and sexual promiscuity; for girls, it includes greater depression, sexual promiscuity, and childbearing at an earlier age than is the social norm. In adolescence, secure infants are expected to display the opposite suite of traits: delayed childbearing, fewer acts of aggression, fewer symptoms of depression, and greater sexual commitment to their girlfriends, boyfriends, or spouses. This theory uses a conditional adaption notion because the two life histories are conditional upon the family life of a child from birth to about five years of age. These early experiences are thought to set the child on one life course or the other; but children in the two groups do not differ genetically—or if they do, the effect of these genetic differences is minor compared to the influence of early experience.

I have been skeptical of this theory, partly because I am skeptical of any theory that makes early experiences the root of adult characteristics, whether proposed by Sigmund Freud (1917), the founder of psychoanalysis, or Mary Ainsworth (1979), a major contributor to the study of infants' emotional attachments. One reason for my skepticism is that behavior is not particularly stable from infancy into adolescence some nine years later. Securely attached infants can have poor outcomes; insecurely attached infants, good ones. Moreover, these outcomes may be a result of heritable traits—such as depressed parents giving birth to children with a genetic risk for insecure attachment and depression. Finally, I believe that the pace of change, even in the Pleistocene, was faster than a 10-year-cycle separating birth and adolescence. A famine, or internecine warfare, could change what might have been a rosy future into a much more miserable one. When the past is no guide to the future, family environmental cues become unreliable. Interested readers can examine my critique of this type of theory (Rowe 2000), a critique by Maccoby (1991), and a rebuttal to Maccoby by Belsky, Steinberg, and Draper (1991b).

Another variant of the conditional adaptation approach is by Cohen and Machalek (1988). The environmental cue in this theory is resource shortages—lack of the money and material goods needed to woo the opposite sex. These shortages are a conditional cue for a lack of *resource holding potential.* Given these conditions, according to the theory, most men will steal and cheat to obtain what they need; these individuals effectively become parasites on the larger, productive economy. This theory, though, is fairly silent about why most individuals growing up in impoverished circumstance fail to resort to criminal acts as a quick fix; it also downplays the poor monetary return on most criminal acts and regards sex differences as more culturally shaped than most evolutionarily based theories do. The interested reader should examine Cohen and Machalek (1988) for more information about their theory.

The Alternative Strategy Theories

Another possibility is that the evolutionary force behind criminal behavior is an alternative strategy: Genes that favor conformity and criminality are kept in some kind of balance in a population. Geneticists call this kind of selective process *frequency dependent selection.* Under frequency dependent selection, a heritable behavior pattern contributes more to fitness when it is rare than when it is common. As it becomes more common, the alternative pattern acquires a higher fitness value. The result is that both patterns can persist in a population, neither one able to drive the other out of existence.

Several of the alternative adaption theories focus on sexual competition as the force maintaining sexually selected alternative strategies in a population. While not explicitly writing about crime, the gifted popularizer of evolutionary biology Richard Dawkins (1976) created a computer model that maintained four behavioral strategies in perpetuity in a population. Two strategies involve loyalty and commitment between romantic partners. The *coy* female insists on a courtship before having sex and is a good parent and wife. The *faithful* male shares these same attributes. As long as the population is composed of just these two types of individuals, most children will be raised in stable, two-parent homes. But the population is in fact unstable, allowing, for instance, for the entry of the *fast* female. She does not insist on a courtship period before sex, so she is able to grab those faithful, good-provider husbands away from the coy females, who do insist on courtship. As fast females become more common after a few generations, they invite the entry of another type of male, the *philanderer,* who is a poor provider and even abandons his children. Philanderer males dislike a courtship period, making them unattractive to coy females; they are, however, attractive to fast females. Now some of those fast females wind up as single mothers, stuck with the uninviting task of raising their children without a husband. This mix of types continues in the population indefinitely, at least within Dawkins's computer model.

A number of alternative strategy theories of crime use this idea of philanderer or "cad" males (Mealey 1995; Rowe 1996; Rowe, Vazsonyi, and Figueredo 1997). Mealey labeled those men genetically inclined toward a life of cheating and crime *primary psychopaths.* These cheaters presumably enjoy a level of reproductive success equal to that of conformers, if they are relatively rare in the population. As they become more common, the reproductive payoff to cheaters is less (i.e., in a world in which most people cheat, the few trustworthy people would gain substantial advantages). Mealey's frequency dependent selection model is comparable to that of the "cad" male and the "dad" male, with the "dad" male describing behaviors similar to those of the faithful male in Dawkins's simulation. In my adaptive strategy theory of crime, I emphasize the relative balance between mating effort—"cad" type behaviors—and parenting effort.

What traits might evolve to support a "cad" style of mating strategy? A strong sexual drive and attraction to the novelty of new sexual partners is clearly one component of mating effort. An ability to appear charming and superficially interested in women while courting them would be useful. The emotional attachment, however, must be an insincere one, to prevent any emotional bonding to a girlfriend or spouse. The cad may be aggressive, to coerce sex from partly willing partners and to deter rival men. He feels little remorse about lying or cheating. Impulsivity could be advantageous in a cad because mating decisions must be made quickly and without prolonged deliberation; the unconscious aim is many partners, not a high-quality partner.

This array of cad personality traits corresponds to those of the psychopath, as described in the psychological literature (Cleckley 1976; Hare 1985, 1991). The psychopath lacks remorse and empathy, is superficially charming and attractive, is selfish and impulsive, pretends intelligence, and is highly exploitative of other people. The psychopath may also be a person with many of the traits of ordinary street criminals but with a bit more impulse control and intelligence. Certainly, these traits are found at a greater prevalence in criminals than in people in the general population. These characteristics may encourage criminal acts that yield so little material return that they often seem self-destructive and nonfunctional (e.g., the average crime nets only a small amount of money), because their real and hidden function is mating success. Most criminal acts involve little planning and satisfy only an immediate, short-term gain. The criminal is impulsive, or in Gottfredson and Hirschi's term, he lacks self-control. The cad, who feels little remorse over emotionally hurting another person, may feel no inhibition against taking another's property, if that's convenient. His greater aggressiveness can encourage acts of violence in a robbery or to maintain his reputation. A cad need not be a criminal; but people high in mating effort traits, given the right opportunities and environmental context, would be more likely than others to resort to a variety of criminal acts. According to Mealey's theory, the primary psychopath is a genetically determined alternative strategy. She contrasts the primary psychopath with the secondary psychopath, an individual who displays many of the same traits as the primary type but developed them because of poor child rearing and antisocial peers (cf. Lykken 1995).

Unlike Mealey, I do not make any sharp distinction between environmental and genetic causation, viewing the genetic influence as increasing quantitatively with higher levels of mating effort. Neither theory gives an explanation for females' criminal behavior, nor for their attraction to criminal men (prisoners sometimes marry females attracted to their notoriety). Mealey's primary psychopath and my alternative strategy theory predict that early experiences in the family are less important for later crime than the conditional adaptation theories hold.

The Evolutionary Perspective: Conclusions

This brief tour of evolutionary approaches to crime can hardly cover all the many subtleties of argument and controversies within the fields using evolution to explain human behaviors. Nor has space permitted covering all the evolutionary perspectives relevant to criminology (cf. Rushton 1995; Ellis and Walsh 1997). All evolutionary theories require a fairly high level of abstraction; they ask about the ultimate source of behaviors—why people behave the way they do. An evolutionary theory does immediately answer many applied questions that concern students of criminology. Does capital punishment deter? Should prisons attempt to rehabilitate criminals? Should we restrict gun sales? Furthermore, traits that are more frequent in criminals than in noncriminals can be described without ever discussing why those traits evolved in the first place. On the other hand, I find it both intellectually satisfying and challenging to think about these broader questions of the ultimate origins of human behaviors.

A problem for evolutionary theories is that they are difficult to prove or disprove. Critics of evolutionary reasoning (Lewontin, Rose, and Kamin 1984) have accused these theories of telling "just so" stories, after Rudyard Kipling's fanciful stories for children (recall that the elephant got its trunk when a crocodile pulled on its nose!). It's easy to generate an adaptive explanation for some odd behavior. My example: The high prevalence of swimming pools in Phoenix, Arizona, is adaptive because the water cools men's sperm, making them more fertile. I lack any evidence for this assertion. I do know, however, that pools pose a danger because children drown in them—making pool owning possibly nonadaptive in the Darwinian sense.

If we had a time machine and could return to early prehistoric times, we could make stronger inferences about the evolution of human traits. Some traits do evolve rapidly; indeed, rather than evolving in the Pleistocene, a cad strategy could have evolved once the development of agriculture in the fertile regions of the world permitted large population sizes and the growth of the first cities. Yet even the records from historical times are too poor to trace the evolutionary history of particular human traits.

Contrary to what many students believe, a theory is more exciting when it can be conclusively disproved—when there is a "counterfactual" to the argument being presented. On these grounds, the evolutionary ones are fairly weak. Yet they are the most exiting and viable theories for exploring the deep roots of human behavior, the wellspring of our humanness. We did evolve from a common ancestor with the chimpanzee about 5 million years ago; this evolutionary history is encoded in our genetic material (DNA). The only way to fully understand behavior is to examine it from an evolutionary perspective, and to find methods to sharpen theories of the evolution of behavior and to apply them more precisely to crime.

Recommended Reading

Daly, M. and M. Wilson. 1988. *Homicide*. New York: Aldine de Gruyter. Daly and Wilson's book is a marvelous tour of evolutionary thinking applied to the ultimate crime: murder.

References

Ainsworth, M. D. S. 1979. "Infant-mother Attachment." *American Psychologist* 34: 932–937.

Alcock, J. 1997. *Animal Behavior: An Evolutionary Approach* (6th ed.). New York: Sinauer Associates.

Belsky, J., L. Steinberg, and P. Draper. 1991a. "Childhood Experience, Interpersonal Development, and Reproductive Strategy: An Evolutionary Account of Socialization." *Child Development* 62: 647–670.

—. 1991b. "Further Reflections on an Evolutionary Theory of Socialization." *Child Development* 62: 682–685.

Berenbaum, S. A. 1996. Personal communication (June).

Berenbaum, S. A. and M. Hines. 1992. "Early Androgens Are Related to Childhood Sex-typed Toy Preferences." *Psychological Science* 3: 203–206.

Buss, D. 1995. *The Evolution of Desire: Strategies of Human Mating*. New York: Basic Books.

—. 2000. *The Dangerous Passion: Why Jealousy Is as Necessary as Love and Sex*. New York: Free Press.

Cleckley, H. 1976 (1941). *The Mask of Sanity.* St. Louis: Mosby.

Cohen, L. E. and R. Machalek R. 1988. "A General Theory of Expropriative Crime: An Evolutionary Ecological Approach." *American Journal of Sociology* 94: 465–501.

Crawford, C. and D. L. Krebs. 1998. *Handbook of Evolutionary Psychology: Ideas, Issues, and Applications.* Mahwah, NJ: Lawrence Erlbaum Associates.

Daly, M. and M. Wilson. 1988. *Homicide.* New York: Aldine de Gruyter.

Dawkins, R. 1976. *The Selfish Gene.* Oxford: Oxford University Press.

—. 1987. *The Blind Watchmaker.* New York: W. W. Norton.

Draper, P. and H. Harpending. 1982. "Father Absence and Reproductive Strategy: An Evolutionary Perspective." *Journal of Anthropological Research* 38: 255–273.

Eibl-Eibesfeldt, I. 1970. *Ethology: The Biology of Behavior.* New York: Holt, Rinehart and Winston.

Ekman, P. 1994. "Strong Evidence for Universals in Facial Expressions: A Reply to Russell's Mistaken Critique." *Psychological Bulletin* 115: 268–287.

Ellis, L. and A. Walsh. 1997. "Gene-based Evolutionary Theories in Criminology." *Criminology* 35: 229–276.

Freud, S. 1917. *Introductory Lectures on Psychoanalysis.* (J. Riviere and J. Strachey, trans., London: Hogarth, 1963).

Gangestad, S. W. and J. A. Simpson. 1990. "Toward an Evolutionary Theory of Female Sociosexual Variation." *Journal of Personality* 58: 69–96.

Gottfredson, M. R. and T. Hirschi. 1983. "Age and the Explanation of Crime." *American Journal of Sociology* 89: 552–584.

Gottesman, I. I. 1991. *Schizophrenia Genesis: The Origins of Madness.* New York: W. H. Freeman.

Hare, R. D. 1985. "Comparison of Procedures for the Assessment of Psychopathy." *Journal of Consulting and Clinical Psychology* 53: 7–16.

—. 1991. *The Hare Psychopathy Checklist, Revised.* Toronto, Ontario, Canada: Multi-Health Systems.

Hollox, E. J., M. Poulter, M. Zvarik, V. Ferak, A. Krause, T. Jenkins, N. Saha, A. I. Kozlov, and D. M. Swallow. 2001. "Lactase Haplotype Diversity in the Old World." *American Journal of Human Genetics* 68: 160–172.

Ingman, M., H. Kessmann, S. Paabo, and U. Gyllensten. 2000. "Mitrochondrial Genome Variation on the Origin of Modern Humans." *Nature* 408: 708–713.

Kanazawa, S. and M. C. Still. 2000. "Why Men Commit Crimes (and Why They Desist)." *Sociological Theory* 18: 434–447.

Lewontin, R. C., S. Rose, and L. J. Kamin. 1984. *Not in Our Genes: Biology, Ideology, and Human Nature.* New York: Pantheon Books.

Lykken, D. T. 1995. *The Antisocial Personalities.* New York: Lawrence Erlbaum Associates.

Lynn, R. 1995. "Dysgenic Fertility for Criminal Behavior." *Journal of Biosocial Sciences* 27: 405–408.

Maccoby, E. E. 1991. "Different Reproductive Strategies in Males and Females." *Child Development* 62: 676–681.

Mealey, L. 1995. "The Sociobiology of Sociopathy: An Integrated Evolutionary Model." *Behavioral and Brain Sciences* 18: 523–599.

Reiss, A. J. and D. P. Farrington. 1991. "Advancing Knowledge About Co-offending: Results From a Prospective Longitudinal Study of London Males." *Criminology* 82: 360–395.

Rowe, D. C. 1996. "An Adaptive Strategy Theory of Crime and Delinquency." In J. D. Hawkins (ed.), *Delinquency and Crime: Current Theories,* pp. 268–314. Cambridge, England: Cambridge University Press.

—. 2000. "Death Hope and Sex: Steps to an Evolutionary Ecology of Mind and Morality." *Evolution and Human Behavior* 21: 352–364.

Rowe, D. C., A. T. Vazsonyi, and A. J. Figueredo. 1997. "Mating Effort in Adolescence: Conditional or Alternative Strategy." *Personality and Individual Differences* 23: 105–115.

Rushton, J. P. 1995. *Race, Evolution, and Behavior.* New Brunswick, CT: Transaction Publishers.

Steffensmeier, D. J., E. A. Allan, M. D. Harer, and C. Streifel. 1989. "Age and the Distribution of Crime." *American Journal of Sociology* 94: 803–831.

Stouthamer-Loeber, M. and E. H. Wei. 1998. "The Precursors of Young Fatherhood and Its Effect on Delinquency of Teenage Males." *Journal of Adolescent Health Research* 22: 56–65.

Tooby, J. and L. Cosmides. 1992. "The Psychological Foundations of Culture." In J. Barkow, L. Cosmides, and J. Tooby (eds.), *The Adapted Mind,* pp. 19–136. New York: Oxford University Press.

Wilson, E. O. 1975. *Sociobiology: The New Synthesis.* Cambridge, MA: Harvard University Press. ✦

Chapter 4

Does the Body Tell? Biological Characteristics and Criminal Disposition

Most people live with the comfortable belief that they are whole and intact and in control of their fate. This belief can be utterly violated when the brain is damaged by a stroke. A stroke localized in one brain area can leave the victim unable to recognize faces. To the stroke victim, a person first seen walking in the door five minutes later looks like a complete stranger. A stroke may make a person able to button his shirt with his left hand but not with his right hand. Another kind of stroke obliterates memory—the person exists in a continually moving present. The stroke patients can hear a conversation after a two-minute pause as though it were new because they lack any recollection of what was just said. The solid foundation of our self-identity depends entirely on the healthy functioning of our brain. From the vantage point of neurological science, there is no dualism between brain and mind: They are one and the same.

Two medical cases have been studied by the neurologist Antonio Damasio and his colleagues that illustrate a possible neurological underpinning for psychopathy (Anderson et al. 1999). Their subjects, a man and a woman, had both suffered injuries to the prefrontal cortex during infancy. The prefrontal cortex, located just behind the eye sockets and above the bridge of the nose, is involved in planning a sequence of actions and in anticipating the future. The female subject was run over by a car when she was 15 months old. The male subject had a brain tumor removed from his prefrontal area when he was 3 months old. Both subjects grew up in stable, middle-class families with college-educated parents and had normal biological siblings, but neither made a satisfactory social adjustment; neither had friends and both were dependent on support from their parents. Neither subject had any plans for the future. The woman was a compulsive liar; she stole from her parents and shoplifted; her early and risky sexual behavior led to a pregnancy by age 18. By age 9, the male subject had committed minor theft and aggressive delinquent acts; he had no empathy for others.

The researchers tested the two subjects on a computerized gambling test used to detect how people respond to the uncertainty of rewards and punishments. The task is designed so that payoffs to the "bad" card deck are high and immediate while payoffs to the "good" card deck are low immediately but better in the long term. Most people quickly learn to draw cards from the "good" deck that offers the better long-term payoff. Neither subject was able to learn to use the long-term payoff deck.

Most surprisingly, these brain-injured victims failed to understand the difference between right and wrong; they lacked a sense of social norms and of how to act in social situations. Their moral blindness contrasts with the thought processes of adults who have brain damage in the same region and who display symptoms of psychopathy but understand without any difficulty the moral difference between right and wrong.

Finding the Physiological Basis of Criminal Disposition

The prefrontal cortex could mediate genetic influence on criminal dispositions if genes affect the functioning of this brain region. In a prominent theory of attention deficit hyperactivity disorder, the same brain region has been implicated (Barkley 1997). Deficits in the prefrontal cortex may reduce the executive function—that is, the ability to plan and to reflect on one's actions. Impaired executive function implies impulsive and disorganized behavior, a focus on the present rather than on the future. Tests involving specific tasks that require executive function can distinguish between psychopaths and control individuals. One is the classic delay-of-gratification task. In one version, a computer screen presents a signal for a 40 percent probability of winning a nickel; the subject can take the nickel or wait 14 seconds for an 80 percent probability of a win (and better long-term winnings). Psychopathic offenders pick the immediate reward more often than nonpsychopathic offenders (Newman, Kosson, and Patterson 1992). Notice that this task presents the same basic situation as Damasio's card deck task: to work for a long-term payoff in the presence of immediate payoffs.

Despite advances in our understanding of the function of brain regions, no diagnostic test for criminal dispositions exists at this time. A brain tumor can be diagnosed unequivocally by brain-imaging technology and a biopsy (sample) of the brain tissue. With diagnostic medical tests, a stress headache can be reliably distinguished from a brain tumor. Although modern brain-imaging technologies can produce wonderfully detailed images of the living, functioning brain, they cannot pick out the criminally disposed from the nondisposed with anything like a diagnostic level of accuracy. Before examining some specific biological risk factors for criminal disposition, we must consider several methodological issues.

Risk Factors Versus Diagnosis

Biological indicators of criminal dispositions have been found. These indicators can be called "risk factors" for crime because their presence increases the chances that a criminal disposition exists. The relation of current biological indicators and criminal disposition is too weak to make a specific diagnosis for a particular person.

Biological measures seem more scientific and certain than questionnaires and other "instruments" used by the social scientist. Yet biological tests are not without their complications. To be useful, a measure must be reliable. A single blood pressure reading, for instance, has low reliability because blood pressure is changed by daily stresses and by the sleep-wakefulness cycle. Doctors must be careful to make a diagnosis of hypertension on the basis of several high blood pressure readings. The reliability statistics of many biological tests used to predict criminal disposition have not been reported in articles; if their reliability is low, biological tests may fail to predict criminal disposition.

To understand the idea of reliability, imagine that players are being selected for a basketball team on the basis of their heights. However, unknown to you, a coaching assistant flips a coin and subtracts four inches from the real height if the reading comes up heads and adds four inches if it comes up tails. The assistant then hands you these falsified height scores. Naturally, more mistaken choices are made with these false scores than with the true ones. The false scores are unreliable; they contain random error from the coin flipping. Of course, if you had known the players' field-goal percentages, you could really pick a winning team, but that's another story.

Causal Direction

Although we want to identify biological dispositions to crime, biological indicators are also influenced by social stimuli. If a bear is running at you, your heart and breathing rate will increase, your blood concentration of the stress hormone cortisol will shoot up, and your palms may start sweating. We do not label these physiological signs a "bear-attack" disposition. The causal direction is from an environmental stimulus to biological response.

More critically, many biological functions respond to environmental stimuli less obvious than an onrushing bear. The male hormone testosterone (*T*) goes up in fans watching their favorite sports teams win; it goes down when the team loses (Bernhardt et al. 1998). Testosterone level also increases after sexual activity (Dabbs and Mohammed 1992). In these examples, the testosterone level soon returns to a baseline level for each individual because the experience does not produce permanent change. Despite the overall heritability of *T*-levels (Harris, Vernon, and Boomsma 1998), a single measurement of *T*-level is not a measure of a biologically based trait only.

The responsiveness of *T*-level to the environment may create a concern about causal direction in associations involving *T*-levels. In a large survey study, however, it is most likely that causal direction is from *T*-level to criminal disposition. Events that strongly affect *T*, like sexual intercourse or a winning sports team, are probably randomly distributed so they would not bias an association. That is, some high-*T* people had sex the night before the survey, but so did some low-*T* people; similarly, a win by the Chicago Bulls basketball team the evening before a survey will increase fans' *T*-levels, but lower the *T*-levels of those who rooted for the other team. Thus, the statistical associations found in a large survey are likely to be causal.

Blood and Saliva Tests of Criminal Disposition

Could we detect criminal disposition with a simple saliva or blood test? There is some positive evidence that a test can be done for some hormones and metabolites of neurotransmitters that circulate in the blood.

Testosterone is the hormone that is responsible for the fetus carrying a *Y* chromosome to develop into a male. It is a biochemical that is simple in structure and that is derived from a substance feared by dieters: cholesterol. *T* attaches to receptors on the surface of specific cells and triggers a cascade of biological events within these cells that ultimately change gene expression in the cell's nucleus; that is, it can turn genes off and on. Testosterone circulates in the blood, a portion free and another portion bound to a carrier protein. Free *T*-levels are inexpensively detectable in saliva (Dabbs et al. 1995). With its powerful physiological effects and its strong connection to masculinity, it is no wonder that men revel in the power of testosterone, as overdramatized in the picture in Figure 4.1.

Two studies have reported on interactions between social integration and the strength of the association between testosterone level and crime in Vietnam veterans; this association was stronger when men's social integration was weaker—that is, when they were of lower social class, were unmarried, or had an unstable work history (Booth and Osgood 1993; Dabbs and Morris 1990). To illustrate, Dabbs and Morris used data on crime and testosterone level in 4,462 Vietnam-era veterans. In their study, higher *T*-level predicted a variety of antisocial behaviors, including aggressive ones. The association was stronger in lower-class men than in middle-class men. Table 4.1 shows the percentage of high-testosterone (upper 10 percent, N = 202) versus

Figure 4.1
Masculinity—An Exaggerated View of the Power of Testosterone

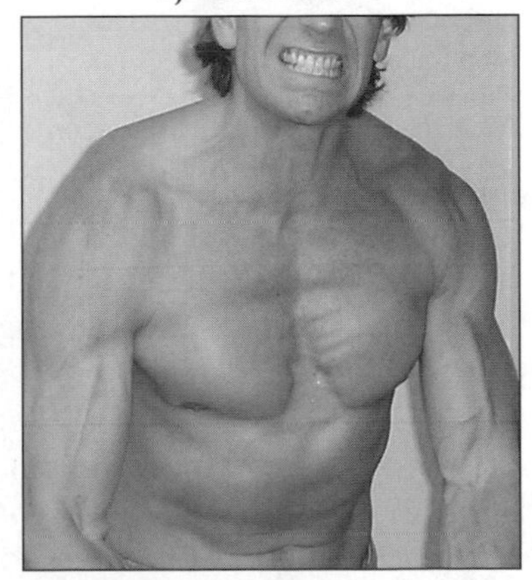

low-testosterone (90th percentile and below; N=1,294) men who were classified as delinquent. Among lower-class men, a higher testosterone level almost doubled the risk of crime, but among the upper-class men, it hardly changed their already low rate of crime. Dabbs and Morris's finding suggests that *T*-level interacts with the social context; it may be a more potent cause of criminal disposition in a lower-class environment. Another possibility is that men who become lower class carry additional genetic risk factors that amplify the effects of testosterone. This second theory gains some credence because the men's class attainment was used, not the social class of their parents.

Other studies of the link between testosterone and crime have been reviewed by Jacobson and Rowe (2000). They noted that the association between testosterone and aggression was more consistent for adults than for adolescents, possibly because of the profound influence of puberty on hormone levels. One study also found the hormone estradiol, a close chemical relative, to be related to females' aggression. Only one research group has examined the association of hormones and female crime, a part of the general neglect of females in studies of crime.

Table 4.1

Percentage of Sample Exhibiting Delinquent Behavior in World War II

	Veterans by Testosterone Level	
	Normal *T* % Delinq.	**High** *T* % Delinq.
Low Social Class	14.7	30.7
High Social Class	4.5	4.1

Note: T = Testosterone. 90 percent of the sample fell into the normal *T* category; 10 percent into the high *T* category.

In adult men, testosterone concentration in saliva has another quite different association that is more appealing than delinquency: a bass voice (Dabbs and Mallinger 1999). The strength of relationship of testosterone level to criminal disposition is about the same as it is to possessing a deep voice. A choir director would not, of course, take blood or saliva samples to find a man ready to sing the bass line in Handel's *Messiah*—the director would audition men to sing instead. Many biological risk factors do not have the specificity to allow them to be used in a strong predictive way to forecast whether a particular individual will in the future commit delinquent acts.

Serotonin Levels

Serotonin is a chemical involved in neurotransmission in the brain. When nerve signals are relayed between sending and receiving nerve cells, serotonin crosses a small gap (the synapse) between one cell and the other and binds to receptor proteins on the surface of the receiving cell. This binding process sets off a biochemical chain reaction that modulates the receiving cell's ability to send further nerve impulses to its target cells. Another molecule, the serotonin transporter protein, has the job of recycling serotonin back into a sending cell for reuse. Serotonin is made from one of the essential amino acids, tryptophan, which is abundant in the American diet, especially in meat. Serotonin originates in cells in a particular region deep in the brain. Like long wires in an electrical circuit, axons from the serotonin-producing nerve cells extend widely throughout the brain, including into the frontal cortex, where they may modulate higher thought processes (Spoont 1992).

Serotonin levels cannot be measured directly by biological test without risking brain damage to the subject. Two indirect methods are thus used; the first involves measuring the level of a serotonin metabolite (SM) in a biochemical pathway that breaks down serotonin in cerebral spinal fluid; the second measures the level of serotonin itself inside blood platelet cells.

A consistent association has been found between low cerebral spinal fluid SM levels and suicidal impulses, suicide attempts, and completed suicides (Asberg 1997). Spinal fluid SM levels are also lower in violent criminals (Fuller 1996). Furthermore, people with suicidal ideation are sometimes impulsively aggressive, and their aggression is associated with lower SM levels.

The serotonin system is the target of a class of antidepressant drugs first discovered about 1975: the serotonin reuptake inhibitors. The most famous of these drugs, fluoxetine, goes under the trade name Prozac. The ability of the drug to relieve major depressive disorder, and seemingly to modify many other personality problems, led to the publication of a best-selling book, *Listening to Prozac* (Kramer 1997). The mechanism of Prozac's action lends further support to the hypothesis linking psychopathology with low serotonin levels. Prozac binds to and thereby blocks the action of the serotonin transporter protein; it is therefore likely that Prozac relieves depression partly by increasing the availability of serotonin in the synapses between cells. On the other hand, this account is certainly an oversimplification of how Prozac works. Prozac also binds to and thereby activates one class of serotonin receptor proteins, and it may have many unknown metabolic effects. In the last chapter, we consider ways in which the antidepressant drugs have become a treatment intervention for criminals.

Figure 4.2

Blood Platelet Serotonin Levels in Male Sample and in Violent Males

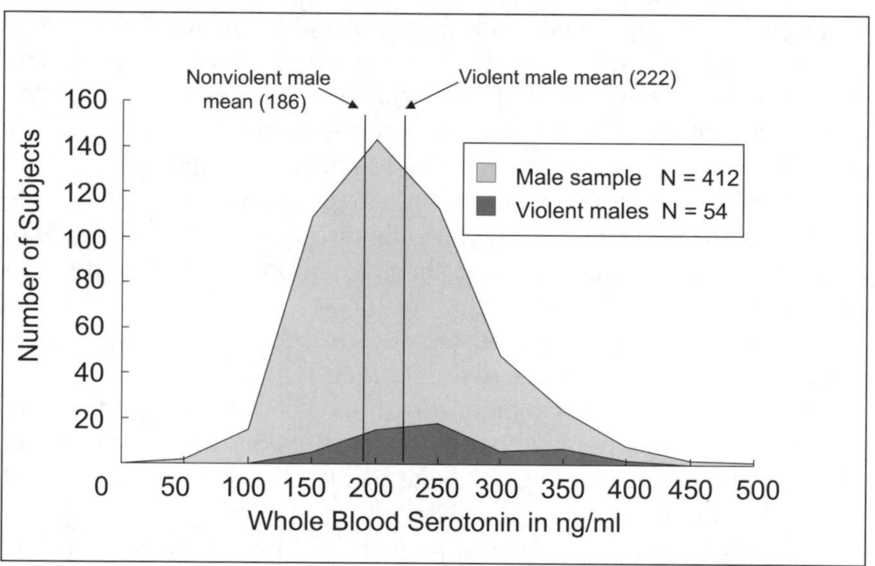

Source: Reprinted from Moffitt, T. E., G. L. Brammer, A. Caspi, J. P. Fawcett, M. Raleigh, A. Yuwiler, and P. Silva. (1998). "Whole Blood Serotonin Relates to Violence in an Epidemiological Study." *Biological Psychiatry* 43, 446–457. Copyright © Society of Biological Psychiatry. Reprinted by permission.

Unlike most previous researchers, Moffitt and her colleagues (1998) used a general population sample instead of a sample of psychiatric patients. They also measured serotonin levels in blood platelet cells. The sample consisted of 781 21-year old men and women, all born in the same year in New Zealand. Violence was measured by using criminal convictions and self-reports of violence. In males, higher levels of platelet serotonin were found to be associated with violence. This effect also held up to statistical controls for possibly related factors such as drug use, platelet count, body mass, psychiatric disorder, social class, nonviolent crime, and family relations. Figure 4.2 shows the distribution of whole blood serotonin levels in violent and nonviolent males. The violent males had a mean blood platelet concentration of 222 ng/ml, versus 186 ng/ml in the rest of the male sample. From these data, we can estimate that the correlation coefficient between serotonin levels and violence as approximately .25.

The two measures of serotonin levels, (in spinal fluid versus in platelets) have opposite relationships to behavior disorders. However, the studies of spinal fluid measure the amount of metabolite after serotonin has been released into the synapse between nerve cells and then used. If the metabolite is low, it means that less serotonin has been available for communicating between nerve cells. The platelet serotonin studies measure the amount of serotonin still stored inside the platelet—the amount that has not yet been released for communication. Thus, if communication between cells is poor, this effect would theoretically result in *high* concentrations of serotonin stored (in neurones or platelet cells) and *low* concentrations released to be converted into a serotonin metabolite (by synapse or muscle), conceptually resolving the opposite direction of the associations found with the two assays.

Heart Rate Tests of Criminal Disposition

Heart rate is a physiological activity that is exquisitely sensitive to many environmental demands. Although the heart is a peripheral organ from the brain, the activity of the brain, including a psychological appraisal of situations, determines heart rate through the nervous system. Heart rate depends on the balance of the activity of the sympathetic and parasympathetic nervous systems; the former increases heart rate while the latter decreases it. Stimuli that grab one's attention first accelerate heart rate in an orienting response. The mental exertion of a game of chess makes the heart beat more rapidly—perhaps chess qualifies as a sport after all. Imagine that you are stepping into a doctor's office or are about to receive a medical exam from a survey interviewer. Unconsciously you will appraise the situation; if it seems mildly threatening, your heart rate may increase—but not by much, if you are someone with a greater criminal disposition than the average person.

In his book on crime as a clinical disorder, Raine (1993) summarized 14 studies of the relationship between resting heart rate and crime. All 14 studies found a lower resting heart rate to be associated with a greater rate of crime. Heart rate was measured from simple pulse counting to sophisticated electrical measurements. Definitions of crime included criminal records, teacher ratings, self-reports on personality tests, and a psychiatric diagnosis of conduct disorder. The association between low heart rate and criminal disposition was found in both American and English samples and in both males and females. The statistical association was also upheld in subsequent studies (Raine et al. 1997). In sum, this finding was particularly robust because it held across samples drawn from different populations and over the various types of heart rate measures.

This association has also been found in studies that follow the same individuals through their lives, with a low heart rate measured well before the onset of criminal behaviors (Farrington 1997; Raine, Venables, and Mednick 1997). Raine et al. examined the association between heart rate when children were age 3 and the same children's antisocial behaviors when they were 11. The study took place on an island of Mauritius in the Indian Ocean, known for its excellent scuba diving. An amazing 100 percent cooperation rate was gained with the local Indian, Creole, and other descent populations by offering mothers two bags of flour, a candy for their children, and a free health screening. Heart rate was measured with a one-minute recording of the pulse. Aggressive and nonviolent antisociality were assessed by parental reports when the children were 11 years old. Those children with lower heart rates were rated as more aggressive than those with higher rates. As shown in Figure 4.3, children with low heart rates age 3 had about twice the prevalence of aggression at age 11, versus those children with high heart rates at age 3. Considered from another vantage, the high-aggression group averaged about seven fewer heartbeats per minute than the low aggression group. Heart rate predicted aggressive acts more strongly than nonaggressive forms of delinquency, and this association also held when statistical controls were introduced for body size and social class.

Farrington's Cambridge Study in Delinquent Development also found a prospective association between low resting heart rate at age 18 and criminal convictions from ages 19 to 40. Among men with very low heart rates (fewer than 60 beats per minute), 17 percent had convictions, versus 5 percent of the men with very high heart rates (81 beats or more per minute). This association held when other variables were statistically controlled, including low verbal IQ, unstable job record, risk taking between the ages of 8 and 10, and parental convictions. Thus, this biological measure improved the prediction of crime.

Figure 4.3
Association Between Heart Rate and Aggression

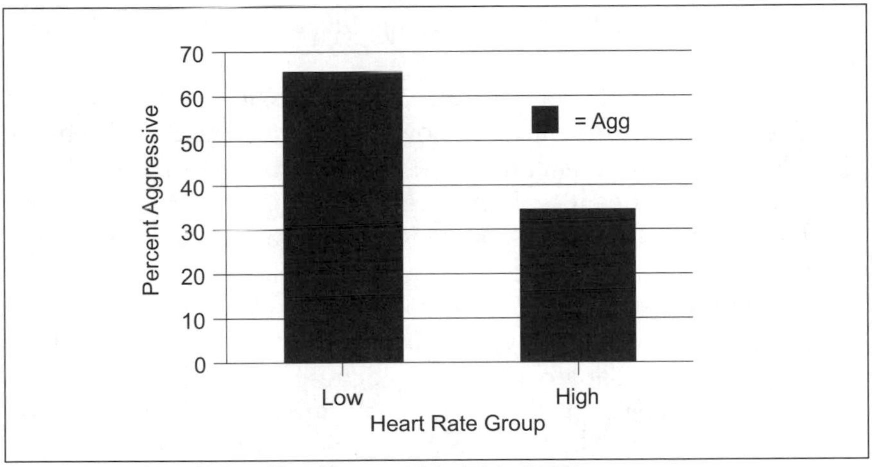

Percent Aggressive
70
60
50
40
30
20
10
0
= Agg
Low
High
Heart Rate Group

Source: Data from Raine, Venables, and Mednick. 1997.

Skin Conductance Tests of Criminal Disposition

Unlike heart rate, which assesses the interaction between the excitatory sympathetic nervous system and the inhibitory parasympathetic nervous system, skin conductance (SC) reflects only the central nervous system's stimulation of the sympathetic nervous system. In the central nervous system, skin conductance can reflect the diversion of attentional resources to a particular stimuli, as when orienting to that stimuli.

Skin conductance is measured by recording how much the fingers sweat. As fluids leak from pores in the skin, they carry ions (charged particles) of chloride and sodium that permit an electrical current to flow; skin conductance is then measured by testing the electrical resistance across wires attached to two fingers.

Associations have been found between a weak skin conductance response and criminal disposition (Raine 1993). However, the research literature on SC response is more mixed than that on resting heart rate. Psychopaths and antisocial individuals tend to be characterized by a weaker resting skin conductance response—measured in the absence of any provoking stimuli, such as a loud noise or speech. Not every study finds this relationship, and the exact reason that some studies are failures and others successful may depend on subtle changes in the test conditions. Criminally-disposed individuals also show a stronger skin conductance half-recovery time. The half-recovery time is the time it takes for skin conductance to return halfway to baseline after a stimulus, but its physiological basis is not well understood.

One underlying factor for both a weaker skin conductance and lower resting heart rate may be a lower state of arousal in the brain. This idea, that lower brain arousal leads to crime, was one of the first physiological hypotheses for criminal behavior (Eysenck and Gudjonsson 1989). Because individuals with a criminal disposition would be in a state of low mental arousal, the mildly threatening situation of a medical test would fail to raise their heart rates. This theory holds that to compensate for a low level of arousal, these individuals seek out activities that are intrinsically arousing. Crimes, such as getting into a bruising fight or threatening someone in a robbery, are physically arousing acts. For a person with a normal level of brain arousal, such acts would increase mental arousal to such an intolerable level that the acts would become psychologically aversive. But for a person with low level of arousal, the same increase of arousal would be pleasantly stimulating and rewarding. In this case, crime is a self-medication for a chronically under aroused brain.

Another interpretation of these physiological findings is an underlying personality characteristic of fearlessness. A lack of fear may account for heart rate and resting skin conductance remaining low in a mildly threatening situation. A lack of fear could also predispose toward crime because fearless children would be more difficult to socialize than fearful ones—punishment would arouse a less intense emotion, and the lesson inadequately learned. It is also better not to be afraid when breaking into a house or threatening violence. As Clint Eastwood intoned in the movie *The Unforgiven*, it is fearlessness that lets the gunslinger shoot straight, not his speed of draw.

Of these two explanations, I favor low arousal over fearlessness. One of my graduate students, Bo Cleveland (1998), included both measures of fearlessness and stimulation seeking in a study of delinquency and sexual coercion. The measure of fearlessness gave uniformly disappointing findings; it correlated neither with crime nor with other measures of criminal disposition. In contrast, the measures that best fit the under arousal theory, scales of impulsiveness and sensation seeking, correlated with crime. My reading of the overall research literature is that impulsivity and sensation seeking are more strongly associated with crime than either anxiety or fearlessness.

On the other hand, the low arousal theory has its limitations. It is hardly an argument for linking physiology specifically to criminal disposition. Low arousal can be relieved through many socially acceptable activities. The NASCAR racer, the high-altitude mountain climber, and the diver exploring an undersea canyon, all have sensation-seeking traits. The low arousal theory is incomplete because it does not indicate why a particular individual turns to crime rather than to adventure. Ideally, a physiological basis of crime would distinguish between these two groups, a level of specificity that has yet to be achieved.

Tests of Brain Anatomy and Function

A technological revolution has made it possible to view the anatomy and function of the living brain with tremendous precision. A variety of brain imaging techniques have opened a whole new window on the mind. One form of brain imaging is *positron emission tomography* (PET) scanning. These scans show which part of the brain is most active during cognitive tasks.

To be PET scanned, you must first be injected with a form of sugar with a radioactive label attached to it. Sugar fuels the brain. The most active regions of the brain draw the most sugar-fuel from the bloodstream, while the less active areas draw in less sugar. This process is dynamic, with sugar utilization rapidly following changes in the level of brain metabolic activity. After receiving your injection of radioactive-labeled sugar, in the typical experiment you would be asked to work on a cognitive task for about half an hour. During this task, the most active brain regions, down to volumes a few millimeters square, would absorb the greatest amount of radioactive sugar.

After completing the task, you would lie down with your head placed in a PET scanner. The radioactively labeled sugar molecules would now be in your brain cells. Their released high-energy positrons can then be detected by the PET scanner and these data would be used by a sophisticated computer program to create a picture of your brain regions according to the intensity of their sugar uptake; this picture thus shows which sections of the brain were most physiologically active. This method of imaging the brain, because it uses a radioactive-labeled sugar and complex equipment, is quite expensive for research use.

In comparison to a PET scan, a *magnetic resonance imaging* (MRI) scan shows brain anatomy more than brain function. As with the PET scanner, the subject lies down inside a large MRI machine and holds his head steady. A powerful magnetic field then rushes through the subject's head, causing hydrogen nuclei, like small spinning tops, to spin in one orientation. The MRI most strongly affects protrons in hydrogen atoms. Hydrogen is one of the most abundant elements in the brain, a component of water (H_20) and of most organic molecules. Once the magnetic field is switched off, the protrons immediately reorient and give off energy in the radio spectrum that is picked up by coils in the MRI machine and translated by a computer program into an exquisitely detailed three-dimensional picture of brain anatomy—one that can be sliced along any plane, as though the brain were cut by a sharp knife and the sections held up for viewing. A modification of the MRI machine, called functional MRI, also provides information about brain activity. These marvelous technologies have greatly aided medical diagnosis and have opened to research the relationship between the mind—mental activity—and the brain, its physical organ.

Raine and his colleagues have explored the relationship between brain images and criminal disposition for more than a decade. Their general finding is that the prefrontal lobes—the brain region most involved in higher thought processes and in the integration of emotions and thought—may malfunction in the brain of criminally disposed individuals. Their earliest work was conducted with PET scanning technology. In their 1993 study, the subjects were 22 California murderers, 20 men and two women; 19 controls were normal subjects matched to the murderers on age and sex. In the murderer group, three individuals were schizophrenic; their matched controls were schizophrenic patients without a history of violence. All subjects completed a PET scan to detect their brain's sugar metabolism and thus its active regions. In the half-hour testing procedure, the subjects identified numerical targets on a computer screen. After the test was completed, they were placed into the PET scanner, and high-energy positrons were used to locate the brain areas of strongest sugar metabolism.

Results from the PET scan are relative ones. Activity in one brain area is expressed relative to activity in all other brain areas. The deficit in murderers, such that their brain activity was lower than the control group's, was relatively specific to the most forward prefrontal areas of the brain, the region behind the forehead. Schizophrenics showed lower than normal activity in the parietal lobe (upper half of the brain above the ear) and temporal lobe (behind the ear). Unlike them, the murderers were no different from controls in their parietal and temporal lobe activity levels. One murderer did not fit the overall pattern. This man was a serial killer with approximately 45 victims over the years. Raine and his colleague speculated that this man planned his crimes—otherwise, he would have been caught long before the 45th victim—and hence he needed normal prefrontal activity for planning and foresight. Raine, Buchsbaum, and LaCasse (1997) extended and replicated these PET scan findings with about twice the number of murderers and controls. They again found a reduced activity level in the prefrontal cortex, as well as abnormal activity levels in deeper brain structures related to aggression.

Why would sugar metabolism be lower in the prefrontal lobes of murderers? One possibility is that the nerve cells themselves differ in the prefrontal region. Perhaps they are less efficient metabolizers of sugar. An alternative hypothesis is that there are fewer nerve cells to uptake sugar, so lower metabolism of sugar would occur in the prefrontal region than in other brain regions. Raine and his colleagues conducted an MRI study that supported this second hypothesis that individuals with criminal disposition differed from controls in their brain anatomy.

In the MRI study, Raine and his colleagues recruited subjects through temporary employment agencies in Los Angeles (Raine et al. 2000). Some employment seekers were diagnosed with antisocial personality disorder (APD) on the basis of a psychiatric interview and a self-report violence scale. Three control groups were constructed from other employment seekers. Subjects in the normal control group had an absence of drug use or psychiatric illness. Those in the drug use control group abused illegal drugs and alcohol but were not antisocial. This control group was included to deal with the high frequency of substance use in the APD group, as Raine wanted to eliminate the possibility that drug abuse had caused brain abnormalities in the APD group. A third control group was created of individuals diagnosed with other psychiatric disorders. In this first brain-imaging study of a nonimprisoned sample of offenders, the subjects were all scanned in an MRI machine.

Figure 4.4 presents a type of brain slice analyzed by Raine's MRI machine. The brain is clearly visible within the outline of the skull. At the surface of the brain, a thin layer of gray matter surrounds a larger layer of white matter. The gray layer consists of nerve cell bodies; the white area, of axons from those nerve cells that, like wires, carry signals to other parts of the brain and body. The MRI findings were extremely specific: The antisocial personality disorder group had lower prefrontal gray matter volumes than any of the three control groups. There was no difference in the volume of the prefrontal white matter. Relative to the normal controls, the APD group had an 11 percent reduction in gray-matter volume. Although this anatomical difference is too subtle to be observed in a cursory radiological examination—only a thickness difference of .5 mm—it is still a substantial statistical effect. The correlation of the ratio, prefrontal gray matter volume to whole brain volume, with APD was about .40.

Figure 4.4
Coronal Slice of the Prefrontal Cortex

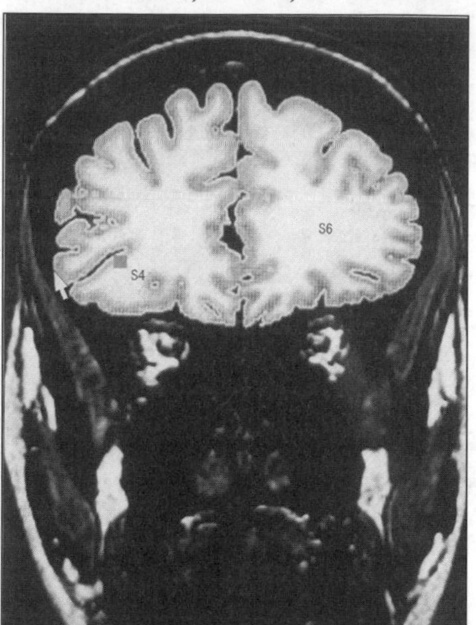

Illustrating areas for the calculation of gray and white volumes. Gray outlines the cerebral cortex and the adjacent gray matter composed of nerve cells; white matter is the lightest shade and is mainly nerve cell axons

Source: Reprinted from Raine, A., T. Lencz, S. Bihrle, L. LaCasse, and P. Colletti. (2000). "Reduced Prefrontal Gray Matter Volume and Reduced Autonomic Activity in Antisocial Personality Disorder." *Archives of General Psychiatry* 57, 119–127. Copyright © American Medical Association. Reprinted by permission.

Conclusions About Biological Tests of Crime

This short chapter can only sample from the many advances in the physiological testing of criminal disposition. Among the omitted topics were the association between crime and electrical activity in the brain (as measured with the electroencephalogram, or EEG); brain evoked potentials; cortisol; and other measures (Fishbein et al. 1989; Susman, Dorn, and Chrousos 1991; see reviews in Raine 1993).

This work on the biological basis of crime differs from that of the nineteenth-century phrenologists. Those scientists sought distinctive physical stigmata that could be used to unequivocally identify criminal individuals and distinguish them from noncriminal ones. The phrenologists looked to physical features, such as large jaws and protrusions on the skull, that would absolutely classify a person as criminal. Their chosen physical markers of criminality turned out not to be associated with criminal disposition. The biologically oriented scientists in this chapter would readily admit that the goal of the phrenologists was an unrealistic one. The criminal mind, and its biology, falls on a continuum with the minds of normal, law-abiding individuals. Some noncriminals will have low resting heart rates, nonsweating hands, and thin gray matter in their prefrontal cortexes, along with other biological markers of criminal disposition. With any single biological test, the identification of criminally disposed individuals is likely to be poor. With a set of biological measures, identification can be improved, but it will still be imperfect. In their MRI study, Raine and his colleagues (2000) also tested their subjects' resting heart rate and skin conductance levels. They could predict whether someone had antisocial personality disorder with 77 percent accuracy, a 27 percent improvement over guessing.

Although much less than the phrenologists had hoped for, this level of accuracy is still a considerable accomplishment with biological tests. Biological tests predict criminal disposition with about the same strength as the best measures of individuals' environmental circumstances—correlations on the order of .20 to .40. Indeed, the biological tests perform considerably better than some environmental indicators, such as social class. Combining biological and social measures may further improve our understanding about who is at risk of becoming criminal.

A more fascinating outcome of biological research, though, is that it pinpoints a type of biological deficit that is involved in criminal dispositions. The deficit appears to lie in impaired functioning of the frontal cortex. This conclusion is consistent with Damasio's stroke victims, Raine's brain imaging, Barkley's theories of hyperactivity, and skin conductance and heart rate findings. Perhaps the nineteenth-century phrenologists were right in one sense. An enlargement of the prefrontal cortex is one of the most distinctive anatomical differences between *Homo sapiens* and our evolutionary kissing cousin, the chimpanzee. The prefrontal cortex may create our knowledge of mind—that other people are themselves thinking about us—and allow us to adjust our behavior to the needs and concerns of others. The prefrontal cortex is also the physiological basis of the executive functions of planning, of delaying the enticing impulses of the present for better outcomes in the future, and of evaluating many behavioral choices instead of just one. The phrenologists may be approximately right: What is disrupted in a criminal disposition are those abilities of the mind that make us most distinctively human.

Recommended Reading

Raine, A. 1993. *The Psychopathology of Crime.* New York: Academic Press. This book belongs on the bookshelf of any student of biology and crime. Raine makes the argument that criminal behavior is a medical disorder requiring a medical instead of a judicial intervention. He also thoroughly reviews studies on the association between biology and crime.

References

Anderson, S. W., A. Bechara, H. Damasio, D. Tranel, and A. R. Damasio. 1999. "Impairment of Social and Moral Behavior Related to Early Damage in Human Prefrontal Cortex." *Nature Neuroscience* 2: 1032–1037.

Asberg, M. 1997. "Neurotransmitters and Suicidal Behavior: The Evidence From Cerebrospinal Fluid Studies." *Annuals of the New York Academy of Sciences* 836: (Dec. 29), 158–181.

Barkley, R. A. 1997. *ADHD and the Nature of Self-control.* New York: Guilford Press.

Bernhardt, P. C., J. M. Dabbs, Jr., J. A. Fielden, and C. D. Lutter. 1998. "Testosterone Changes During Vicarious Experiences of Winning and Losing Among Fans at Sporting Events." *Physiology and Behavior* 65: 59–62.

Booth, A. and D. W. Osgood. 1993. "The Influence of Testosterone on Deviance in Adulthood: Assessing and Explaining the Relationship." *Criminology* 31: 93–117.

Cleveland, H. H. 1998. *Sexual Coercion: Evolutionary Approaches and Peer Group Contexts.* Unpublished dissertation, University of Arizona.

Dabbs, J. M., Jr., B. C. Campbell, B. A. Gladue, A. R. Midgley, M. A. Navarro, G. Read, E. J. Susman, L. M. Swenkels, and C. M. Worthman. 1995. "Reliability of Salivary Testosterone Measurements: A Multicenter Evaluation." *Clinical Chemistry* 41: 1581–1584.

Dabbs, J. M., Jr. and A. Mallinger. 1999. "High Testosterone Levels Predict Low Voice Pitch Among Men." *Personality and Individual Differences* 27: 801–804.

Dabbs, J. M., Jr. and S. Mohammed. 1992. "Male and Female Salivary Testosterone Concentrations Before and After Sexual Activity." *Physiology and Behavior* 52: 195–197.

Dabbs, J. M., Jr. and R. Morris. 1990. "Testosterone, Social Class, and Antisocial Behavior in a Sample of 4,462 Men." *Psychological Science* 1: 209–211.

Eysenck, H. J. and G. H. Gudjonsson. 1989. *The Causes and Cures of Criminality*. New York: Plenum.

Farrington, D. P. 1997. "The Relationship Between Low Resting Heart Rate and Violence." In A. Raine, P. A. Brennan, D. P. Farrington, and S. A. Mednick (eds.), *Biosocial Bases of Violence*. (pp. 158–183). New York: Plenum.

Fishbein, D. H., R. I. Herning, W. B. Pickworth, C. A. Haertzen, J. E. Hickey, and J. H. Jaffe. 1989. "EEG and Brainstem Auditory Evoked Response Potentials in Adult Male Drug Abusers With Self-reported Histories of Aggressive Behavior." *Biological Psychiatry* 26: 595–611.

Fuller, R. W. 1996. "The Influence of Fluoxetine on Aggressive Behavior." *Neuropsychopharmacology* 14: 77–81.

Harris, J. A., P. A. Vernon, and D. I. Boomsma. 1998. "The Heritability of Testosterone: A Study of Dutch Adolescent Twins and Their Parents." *Behavior Genetics* 28: 165–171.

Jacobson, K. C. and D. C. Rowe. 2000. "Nature, Nurture, and the Development of Criminality." In J. F. Sheley (ed.), *Criminology: A Contemporary Handbook*, 3rd ed., pp. 323–347. New York: Wadsworth.

Kramer, P. D. 1997. *Listening to Prozac*. New York, NY: Penguin Books.

Moffitt, T. E., G. L. Brammer, A. Caspi, J. P. Fawcett, M. Raleigh, A. Yuwiler, and P. Silva. 1998. "Whole Blood Serotonin Relates to Violence in an Epidemiological Study." *Biological Psychiatry* 43: 446–457.

Newman, J. P., D. Kosson, and C. M. Patterson. 1992. "Delay of Gratification in Psychopathic and Nonpsychopathic Offenders." *Journal of Abnormal Psychology* 101: 630–636.

Raine, A. 1993. *The Psychopathology of Crime: Criminal Behavior as a Clinical Disorder*. New York: Academic Press.

Raine, A., M. Buchsbaum, and L. LaCasse. 1997. "Brain Abnormalities in Murders Indicated by Positron Emission Tomography. *Biological Psychiatry* 42: 495–508.

Raine, A., M. S. Buchsbaum, J. Stanley, S. Lottenberg, L. Abel, and S. Stoddard. 1993. "Selective Reductions in Prefrontal Glucose Metabolism in Murderers." *Biological Psychiatry* 36: 365–373.

Raine, A., T. Lencz, S. Bihrle, L. LaCasse, and P. Colletti. 2000. "Reduced Prefrontal Gray Matter Volume and Reduced Autonomic Activity in Antisocial Personality Disorder. *Archives of General Psychiatry* 57: 119–127.

Raine, A., C. Reynolds, P. H. Venables, and S. A. Mednick. 1997. "Biosocial Bases of Aggressive Behavior in Childhood: Resting Heart Rate, Skin Conductance Orienting, and Physique." In A. Raine, P. A. Brennan, D. P. Farrington, and S. A. Mednick (Eds.), *Biosocial Bases of Violence*, pp. 107–126. New York: Plenum Press.

Raine, A., P. H. Venables, and S. A. Mednick. 1997. "Low Resting Heart Rate at Age 3 Years Predisposes to Aggression at Age 11 Years: Evidence From the Mauritius Child Health Project. *Journal of the American Academy of Child and Adolescent Psychiatry* 36: 1457–1464.

Spoont, M. R. 1992. "Modulary Role of Serotonin in Neural Information Processing: Implications for Human Psychopathology." *Psychological Bulletin* 112: 330–350.

Susman, E. J., L. D. Dorn, and G. P. Chrousos. 1991. "Negative Affect and Hormone Levels in Young Adolescents: Concurrent and Predictive Perspectives. *Journal of Youth and Adolescence* 20: 167–190. ✦

Chapter 5

A Gene for Crime? Molecular Genetics and Criminal Disposition

A man in a rather unusual Dutch family had a history of violent outbursts. At the age of 23, he was convicted of raping his sister. He was imprisoned in an institution for the criminally insane, where he got into fights with other inmates. At age 35, after he had been told to finish his work, he stabbed a prison warden in the chest with a pitchfork. In the same family, another man who was criticized for his poor performance tried to run over his supervisor with a car at the sheltered workshop where he worked. Another affected family member forced his sisters to disrobe at knife point. Two men in the family were known arsonists. Needless to say, in this extended family, the teenage girls felt insecure when at home alone with their brothers.

When the geneticist Brunner drew a six-generation pedigree (family tree) of the Dutch family (Brunner et al. 1991), he saw that only male family members were affected with violent outbursts and mild mental retardation; the females were normal. This pattern of inheritance suggested a sex-linked gene that resides on the X chromosome, like red color blindness in males. Through a technique called genetic linkage analysis, Brunner narrowed the gene to a particular region of the X chromosome. With further work, he isolated the gene itself (Brunner et al. 1993). The gene, he discovered, coded for an enzyme called monoamine oxidase A (MAOA) that is responsible for breaking down the neurotransmitters serotonin (see chapter 4) and norepinephrine into by-products, which are then removed from the body. In this particular family, a mutation in the MAOA gene rendered it nonfunctional so that no enzyme was produced. Clearly, other biochemical pathways compensated for the absence of MAOA, as the men had been born and did not die, but the absence of the enzyme was devastating enough to affect their mental ability and vio lence proneness.

Such findings have led some writers in the popular press to overemphasize genetic influence. Soon after Brunner's discovery, newspapers were proclaiming the discovery of a "gene for crime," while ignoring the reality that a disruption of MAOA dealt a blow to thinking as well as to law-abidingness. Furthermore, to date, this gene abnormality has been found only in this one Dutch family, meaning that it is very rare. A single gene may be an explanation for the occurrence of crime in this one family, but it is not one for crime in most families.

Robert Plomin (1994) has coined the memorable acronym OGOD for genetic abnormalities like this one: One Gene, One Disease. There are literally hundreds of single-gene disorders, and some traits also exist that are OGOD but that are not abnormalities, such as the ability to taste a bitter substance called PTC. The influence of genes on complex traits is much more subtle and interactive than it is for diseases determined by changes in a single gene. To describe how a single gene can influence criminal disposition, I must first take a short detour into the basic biology of genes.

An Introduction to Molecular Genetics

From TV shows to high school biology, most people have some familiarity with deoxyribonucleic acid (DNA), the chemical code of life, and with genes. A chromosome is but a single molecule of DNA that has a double-helix shape. On the outside is a backbone structure of chemicals; on the inside are its four bases, adenine (A), thymine (T), guanine (G), and cytosine (C). These bases bind to one another—a weak bond, like a velcro pocket flap. The two bases represented by the curvy letters, G and C, bind to each other, as do the two bases represented by more angular letters, T and A. Figure 5.1 gives one illustration of a tiny part of a whole DNA molecule.

Figure 5.1
Double-Stranded Structure of the DNA molecule

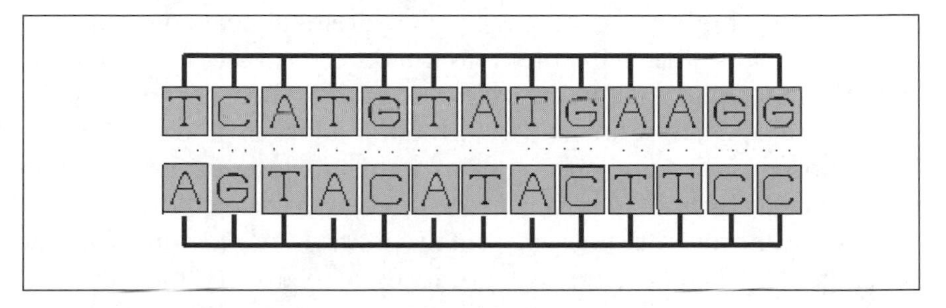

A gene is merely a sequence of bases in the DNA molecule. The following bases could form part of a gene: ATCTTGAGGGCTTAT. Of course, most genes are longer than just 15 bases. The coding region of the typical gene—that is, that part that becomes a protein—is on average 1,200 bases long. Three adjacent bases, such as ATC in the above string of bases, code for amino acids. In nature, there are 20 amino acids, the building blocks of nearly all proteins. The gene basically instructs the body as to which amino acids to link together to make a protein. One might think of amino acids as small Lego blocks of different colors. Each three letters in a row in a gene tells the body which Lego blocks—that is, which amino acid—to pick up and snap together to form a protein. A gene must have a "reading frame" to know where to start to read the meaning of a string of bases. For example, if we started at the beginning of the string, we would read ATC, TTG, AGG, and so on. If the first A were ignored, we would read TCT, TGA, GGG, and so on. The machinery that reads genes is helped by the fact that genes always start with one set of three letters: TAC. Other signals also exist in a gene sequence that help to indicate where genes start and end.

In most higher organisms, there is another complexity to gene structure. The parts of a gene that code for amino acids are broken up by strings of bases that do not code for anything. The former are called *exons*; the latter, *introns*. For this reason, most human genes are much longer than 1,200 bases.

Except for the calcium in our bones, nearly all structural and biochemical functions in the body are served by proteins. You may be familiar with a protein that is the major component of egg white: albumin. Or the one that powers muscles: myosin. Or the protein that carries oxygen in the blood: hemoglobin. Other proteins are involved in chemical reactions. Protein enzymes catalyze chemical reactions between other substances in the body so that they proceed at a proper rate at body temperature. Other proteins are called regulatory proteins because they can enter into the nucleus of a cell and bind to the DNA. Regulatory proteins have a powerful effect because, by sitting on the DNA, they are able to turn other genes on and off. A regulatory protein is like a conductor of an orchestra; just as the conductor coordinates the music of many orchestra players, the cellos with the violins and horns, a regulatory protein controls the action of many other genes. Thus, a gene that produces a regulatory protein may have a stronger than typical impact on development. When one such gene is inappropriately expressed in the fruit fly, the hapless fly grows an extra eye on its wing. Eyes are created by the coordinated action of hundreds of genes; what this regulatory gene does is turn on the eye-creation genes within the wrong body part.

Box 5.1

From the Gene to Protein

The central dogma of molecular biology is that genes code for proteins. Figures 5.2a and 5.2b illustrate this process. The biology of this process has two steps. The first step is named *transcription*. In this step, a gene is copied onto a molecule that is similar to DNA but that is single stranded, not doubled stranded like DNA with its two backbones. It's as though the cell is making a backup copy of its DNA on the A-drive of its computer because it's probably safer for the cell not to use its precious DNA in other metabolic processes. The information-carrier molecule, called ribonucleic acid (RNA), migrates out of the nucleus of the cell into the cytoplasm. RNA that was copied from noncoding parts of DNA, such as introns, is cut out, much as a book editor would strike away unnecessary passages. In Figure 5.2a, the DNA molecule is represented by the darker squares showing the four bases, while the RNA molecule is represented by the white squares. In RNA, uracil (U) substitutes for thymine (T); hence, the code is slightly different. Notice that the RNA molecule is just a single strand of bases.

The second step of the process, *translation,* occurs on ribosomes, structures in the cell devoted to making proteins. This step is shown in Figure 5.2b. Each of the three bases of RNA (here referred to as messenger RNA, or mRNA) corresponds to one of the 20 amino acids, or to a stop signal indicating that the protein is complete. In the figure, the first two amino acids of the protein are already assembled; they are *met*—methionine—and *tyr*—tyrosine. A third amino acid is being added to the growing protein, *glu*—glutamate. These amino acids are chemically bonded to one another in a growing chain, like Lego blocks of assorted colors being snapped together. The average protein contains about 1,200 amino acids, so only a small part of a protein is illustrated in Figure 5.2. Once the protein is complete, it falls away from the ribosome and acquires its functional role in the cell.

Figure 5.2a
One Side of the DNA Molecule Copied Onto Messenger RNA

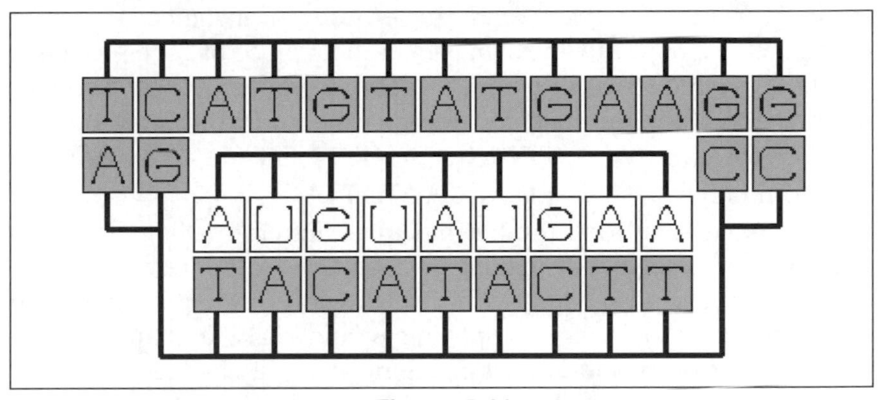

Figure 5.2b
mRNA Translated Into Amino Acids of a Growing Protein

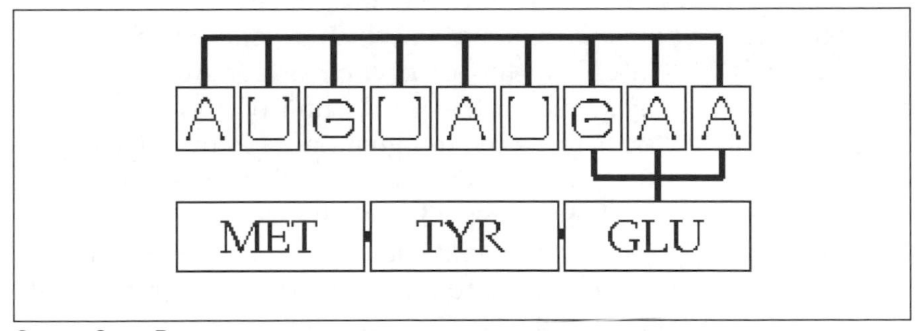

Source: Scott Rowe.

Variation at the Level of the Gene

In chapter 2, I presented some of the methods of behavioral genetics. As a field, behavioral genetics focuses on genetic differences among individuals. I was fairly vague about the exact structure of those genetic differences–something about genes is different, and those differences could affect behavior.

Molecular geneticists have now given us a detailed understanding of variations at the level of the gene. Variants of a gene are called *alleles*, and a gene is said to be *polymorphic* (*poly* = many, *morphic* = forms) when the rarer allele has a frequency of 1 percent or higher, and the more common allele has a frequency of 99 percent or lower. For example, a gene is polymorphic if, when we count 200 genes, 10 are allele A1 and 190 are allele A2.

Several kinds of common variants exist at the level of the gene. One kind is called a *single nucleotide polymorphism*, or SNP. This variant is the result of a change in a single base; for instance, a T could change to a G, or a C to an A. Imagine a short piece of gene sequence in Joe. One sequence is on Joe's chromosome inherited from his mother; the other, on the chromosome inherited from his father:

From mother TTTAGC**CATGTTACG**
From father TTTAGC**AATGTTACG**

The gene from Joe's mother has three letters spelling CAT. The one base pair change, CA, in the gene from Joe's father ruins the spelling of CAT, instead spelling AAT. If this region of the gene is coding for a protein, this change in spelling would make a change in the amino acid from histidine to asparagine. Such a change may seem slight, but it could mean that the protein made by the father's chromosome is nonfunctional. Indeed, in certain unusual genes, only the gene copy from the father (or mother) produces a protein (from a process called genomic imprinting, in which a gene inherited from one parent is turned off). In this case, a devastating disease could result if a base change stopped the production of a protein. As an actual example, an allele given the designation E4 in the APOE gene increases the risk of Alzheimer's disease. The difference between it and the commoner and protective E3 allele is a change in the 134th base of the gene, from adenine (A) in allele E3 to guanine (G) in allele E4 (Ridley 1999, 263). This substitution results in a change in a single amino acid. (SNPs in noncoding regions of a gene also can have functional consequences for how much protein product is made, but I will not detail these mechanisms.)

Another person, say Bill, might have a different genetic makeup. Unlike Joe, who is heterozygous (i.e., carries two different alleles), Bill might be homozygous (i.e., has two alleles that are the same) for the less well-functioning AAT allele, with the genotype:

From mother TTTAGC**AATGTTACG**
From father TTTAGC**AATGTTACG**

Because he has two copies of a less than optimal gene, Bill might suffer from a physical disorder.

Another kind of polymorphism is a repeat of DNA bases. One type of repeat is referred to as the *short-tandem repeat,* or STR. STRs are usually only a few base pairs long; common lengths are two, three, and four base pairs. Thus, one allele is physically a little longer than another. This length difference hardly matters at the scale of the whole chromosome, however, because a chromosome is millions of bases long; an extra 20 bases here, and a fewer 10 bases there, would be unnoticeable on the scale of a whole chromosome.

A CAG repeat is known to cause Huntington's disease, a severe neurological disorder that inevitably results in death (Ridley 1999, 55). An affected individual has an expanded number of repeats, more than 35, sometimes as many as 100. Most normal individuals have 10 to 15 repeats. The CAG repeat exists in the coding region of the Huntington's disease gene; thus, an unaffected person has a length of the same amino acid repeated about 15 times; an affected individual has it repeated many more times. Huntington's disease is dominant because having one "bad" allele with too many CAG repeats is enough to cause the full-blown disease. Not all repeat differences are as dramatic as this one. One allele might have just seven repeats of a base sequence, another eight, as in this example:

From mother:

AGC**CAGCAGCAGCAGCAGCAGCAGCAG**TTC
(eight repeats)

From father:

AGC**CAGCAGCAGCAGCAGCAGCAG**TTC
(seven repeats)

In other cases, the repeat is longer than just a few bases. In one part of the dopamine D4 gene, a gene that has been extensively examined in psychiatric genetics, there is a repeat that is 48 base pairs long. In another gene, the dopamine transporter gene, there is a repeat 40 base pairs long. Polymorphisms composed of these longer repeats are sometimes called VNTRs, for *variable number tandem repeats.* Repeat polymorphisms in noncoding regions of genes also appear to affect their function, such as by determining how much protein is made from a gene (Comings 1998). STR markers are also used in forensic analysis.

Box 5.2

Forensic Analysis

In Miami, a suspected rapist spit onto a sidewalk. A policeman who was following him picked up the spit on absorbent material. The sample was sent to a lab, where the DNA was extracted from cheek cells in the collected saliva. A match was found between the DNA in the criminal's spit and DNA taken from a sperm sample found in a rape victim, leading to the suspect's quick arrest.

Forensic analysis with DNA involves identifying of criminals and excluding innocent people suspected of a crime. Forensic analysis began with fingerprinting. A discovery of Francis Galton, the first behavioral geneticist (see chapter 1), fingerprints are unique to each individual. When a fingerprint "lifted" from a crime scene matches that of a particular individual, it is excellent proof that he or she is perpetrator of a crime. Fingerprints remained the main forensic crimefighting tool for over a hundred years.

Forensic DNA analysis arrived in criminalistics in the 1990s. Its principal method is to have blood or saliva samples gathered at the crime scene genotyped for several short tandem repeat (STR) polymorphisms and compare the results to samples from suspects. STR polymorphisms typically have five to 15 different repeat-size alleles. No two people are likely to possess the same genotypes for several STR polymorphisms (genetic markers). Thus, with four markers, we might exclude a possible murderer if blood collected at the scene and the suspect had the following genotypes:

STR Marker	Suspect Genotype	Crime Scene Genotype
1	A1A6	A12A13
2	A7A5	A3A5
3	A9A14	A3A7

If all the genotypes were the same, however, a match would exist between the criminal suspect and the crime scene sample. Because STRs are highly variable, it varies from unlikely to nearly impossible to have this match happen by chance. Just as no two people have the same fingerprints, STR genetic markers are unique to each person.

Genes and the Determination of Behavioral Characteristics

There is a curious causal asymmetry between genes and behavior. Behavior can affect the expression of genes, whether they are turned off or on, or their level of activity. When a mosquito takes in a blood meal, genes in its gut turn on and become active to produce proteins that digest that blood. Psychological stress can alter gene expression by increasing the level of a hormone, cortisol, that regulates gene expression. Thus, what is going on genetically depends on the environment, and what the genes do may also affect the environment (as when a hungry mosquito goes out and seeks its victim).

Nevertheless, there is an odd asymmetry in that environmental events—except very rare events such as a mutation due to radiation—do not change a gene's DNA sequence. The mosquito's blood meal will not change the DNA sequence of those genes that became activated during its digestion. This fact has two implications. The first is that inheritance is not Lamarckian. The eighteenth-century naturalist Jean de Lamarck incorrectly theorized that acquired characteristics can be inherited. In practical terms, working out at the gym, even though it activates genes in muscle tissue, will not give your son or daughter a genetic head start on acquiring strength. The second implication is that a gene's social environmental direction of causation is more plausible than the reverse. For instance, if it were discovered that for a particular gene teenagers with a seven-repeat allele hung out with delinquent friends more than those with a five-repeat allele, it is more plausible that the allele created a tendency to choose delinquent friends than the reverse; hanging around with delinquent friends will not change a person's repeat number from five to seven.

Methods of Finding Genes Related to Behavioral Traits

Several methods are commonly used to locate genes related to behavioral traits. In this section, I give a brief overview of these methods. For a more extended discussion, see the recommended reading.

Genetic Linkage Analysis

In genetic linkage analysis, a single gene is followed through a family pedigree along with a disorder phenotype (Ott 1999). For example, suppose that in an extended pedigree, we find that the eight-repeat allele of a gene on chromosome 15 occurs in three sons, one parent, and one grandparent, each of whom had a diagnosis of attention deficit hyperactivity disorder (ADHD). One nephew has ADHD, but he also inherited a five-repeat allele. This is pretty good evidence that the eight-repeat allele is "linked" to ADHD. The linkage is imperfect because one child was affected but carried the five-repeat allele instead of the eight-repeat allele. We would conclude that somewhere on chromosome 15, lying close to our STR genetic marker, another change exists in the DNA that makes a child more likely to have ADHD.

Articles in the popular press often misinterpret such genetic linkage findings. In the early 1990s, a reported linkage on the X chromosome between STR genetic markers and homosexuality was called in the popular press "a gene for homosexuality" (Hamer et al. 1993). Now, assuming that this genetic linkage is correct (it has been controversial), it still does not identify a "gene for" homosexuality, because linkage analysis can identify only a *region* in the X chromosome in which this gene might exist.

Genetic Association Analysis

Genetic association analysis is usually done with candidate genes that are hypothesized to influence a phenotype directly (Owen, Cardno, and O'Donovan 2000). Most candidate genes in psychiatry are understood from studies of the actions of drugs that block or enhance neurotransmitters. Many neurotransmitter molecules are known, such as serotonin, as well as the receptor proteins to which they attach and the transporter proteins that regulate their presence in synapses, making genes in these biological pathways prime candidates for studies of behavior.

The logic of an association study is a simple comparison of genotyped people with and without a characteristic. For instance, a study might be done that compares 100 men with criminal records to 100 control men, of similar racial group and socioeconomic level, without any history of crime. A genetic association exists when one allele of a candidate gene is more common in the convicted men than in the control men. Each man carries two copies of a gene (one inherited from each parent). Thus, 100 men have 200 alleles (gene copies). Suppose we find a SNP marker that changes a T to a C. Designate the gene with the T allele as allele A1 and that with C as allele A2. Imagine we obtain the results shown in Table 5.1. Allele A2 occurs 73 times in the criminal men but only 44 times in the noncriminal men. Thus, these numbers show a genetic association. Ideally, this change from T to C is functional; it causes a change that has a physiological effect responsible for an increased risk of criminal behavior. (The change could have had other effects as well on unrelated body systems; for example, it might also raise blood pressure.) If not so, the true functional part of the gene is probably very close to the place in which the T/C change has been located.

Table 5.1

A Hypothetical Association Between a Candidate Gene and Criminal Behavior

Allele	Criminal Men No. Alleles	Control Men No. Alleles
A1 (T)	127	156
A2 (G)	73	44
Total alleles	200	200

Genetic association analysis has one pitfall. A gene may be more common in one group than another because of their genetic heritage, which may be unrelated to the characteristic that is under study. This problem has been called the "chopsticks gene" by Hamer and Sirota (2000) because irrelevant genes, like chopsticks use, may differ in frequency between groups. Chinese people eat with chopsticks while the Irish use knives and forks. Thus, in a combined group of Chinese and Irish, the "chopsticks gene" would show a statistical association with any characteristic that differs in frequency between them; for example, the frequency of red hair would show a negative correlation with the "chopsticks gene," because red hair is more common among the Irish than among the Japanese, and the reverse holds for chopsticks usage. Even Europeans from different places, such as Ireland versus Italy, have somewhat different ancestry, so an association test on a combined Irish and Italian sample could give a false signal because of the ethnic group difference in gene frequencies.

Geneticists have various methods for controlling for this bias in association studies. One easy method is to match the cases and controls on ethnic ancestry; if the cases are Irish, make the controls Irish as well. Another method uses the transmission disequilibrium test, as described in the accompanying box below.

Box 5.3

The Transmission Disequilibrium Test

A clever and simple test of the influence of a single gene is the transmission disequilibrium test (TDT) (Spielman and Ewens 1996). Let's assume a gene with two alleles: A1 is the normal allele; A2 contributes to the likelihood of a psychiatric disorder. Families would be sampled through an affected child, say a child with attention deficit hyperactivity disorder. In a lab, the genotypes of the child, the child's mother, and the child's father are determined. The families in which both parents genotype as homozygous are put aside and not used, as at least one parent must be a heterozygote. Consider eight families in which fathers are heterozygous—that is, they carry the A1 and A2 alleles, and the mothers are A1A1 homozygous:

ADHD Child's Genetic Makeup

	Result 1	Result 2
Family 1	A1A1	A1A2
Family 2	A1A1	A1A2
Family 3	A1A1	A1A2
Family 4	A1A1	A1A2
Family 5	A1A2	A1A2
Family 6	A1A2	A1A2
Family 7	A1A2	A1A2
Family 8	A1A2	A1A1

The mother can pass on to her child only the A1 allele. The father can pass on the A1 allele or the disorder-risk A2 allele. Ordinarily, which gene the father will pass onto his child is as likely as a coin flip. The coin flip outcome is shown in Result 1: Half the time the father passed on A1; the other half, A2. Just as a coin flip does not always come out exactly half heads and half tails, sometimes a father might pass on fewer or more A2 alleles. Result 2, however, is exceptional. Seven of the eight transmissions are of the A2 allele. This is evidence that A2 is a cause of the ADHD disorder. Thus, the TDT test works by looking for an excess transmission of one allele from heterozygous parents to their affected children.

Specific Genes Related to Criminal Disposition

As I emphasized in the introduction, no OGOD genes exist for criminal disposition: No single gene can deterministically make a person into a criminal. Instead, complex traits are subtly influenced by a great number of genes, the exact number of which is unknown. We are living in a time of discovery of those genes related to complex characteristics, but the work is difficult and progress is relatively slow. There have been some successes in the medical field, such as the discovery of important genes related to Alzheimer's disease and breast cancer (Ridley 1999).

Broadly defined, some genes have been discovered with a likely relationship to criminal disposition. In this section, I present several examples of these genes. However, this area is a fast-moving one. New genes will be discovered in the future that may turn out to have a stronger association with criminal disposition than genes currently known; some genes in the current batch of candidate genes may be false leads. I believe that it is certain, though, that as more genes are related to criminal disposition, they will play a greater role in scientific studies and may give a direction to the development of new medical treatments.

The Dopamine Receptor (D4) Gene

Dopamine is a neurotransmitter involved in reward pathways in the brain (Blum et al. 1996). In lab rats, electrical simulation of dopamine nerve cells deep in the brain results in their feeling deeply rewarded; the rats like to repeat the electrical stimulation over and over, their paws pressing a lever for a powerful brain reward, and they prefer it over other enjoyable activities, such as sex. Cocaine, a drug that produces a powerful euphoric high in humans, also acts on dopamine metabolism in the brain.

A well-studied gene and its corresponding protein in the dopamine pathway is the dopamine D4 receptor. The D4 protein resides in the membrane of nerve cells; when dopamine attaches to the receptor, it increases the chances that the nerve cell will fire an electrical signal. Part of the protein resides outside the cell—where dopamine floating in the synaptic gap can latch onto it—and part resides within the cell, where the receptor interacts with other signaling proteins. Inside the cell, the protein can have a long form of seven repeats, each one 48 base pairs long, or a short form of four repeats, each one 48 base pairs long. Because these repeats exist in one of the gene's coding regions (exons), they either add or subtract 16 amino acids. Other, rarer repeat numbers exist in the D4 gene, but I do not consider this complication further.

This D4 receptor gene first came to the attention of behavioral scientists when an association was reported between greater novelty seeking and the seven-repeat allele (Ebstein et al. 1996). The subjects were Israeli college students. On a personality test, those students who had the seven repeat allele had higher novelty-seeking scores than students without this allele. A number of studies have attempted to replicate this finding; some failed to do so, while others have had positive results. Given the many differences among studies in subjects' age and ethnicity, as well as in the sampling procedure, it is difficult to pinpoint a specific cause of the failures to replicate. Some failures may merely reflect the reality that the association is not strong; the seven-repeat allele is more a nudge in the direction of novelty seeking than a strong cause. The seven-repeat allele has also been associated with insecure attachment in infancy (Lakatos et al. 2000).

In the realm of behavior disorders, fairly consistent evidence exists for an association between attention deficit hyperactivity disorder (ADHD) in childhood, which is an antecedent of crime, and the seven-repeat allele (Faraone et al. 2001). After reviewing all published and unpublished studies up to about early 2000, Faraone and colleagues concluded that an association between D4 and ADHD existed in both case-control studies comparing ADHD children to control children and within-family studies (see Box 5.3 on page 100 on the transmission disequilibrium test). In one within-family study (Sunohara et al. 2000), transmissions of the seven-repeat allele to children diagnosed with ADHD were counted. The seven-repeat allele was transmitted to an affected child 75 times and not transmitted 47 times. If this allele had no relationship to ADHD, the expectation would be transmitted 61 times and not transmitted 61 times. Thus, the seven-repeat allele was more likely to pass from a heterozygous parent who carried it to an affected child, implying that it is a contributory influence on ADHD.

In my lab's work on ADHD, I discovered an association between ADHD, especially the inattention component, and the seven-repeat allele (Rowe et al. 1998). My study involved both case and control parents and their children. In another study using this sample (Rowe et al. 2001), I analyzed the parents' retrospective (to the teenage years) reports of conduct disorder (CD). (If you do not prefer to use psychiatric terminology, you can regard the retrospective CD scale as a self-report delinquency scale.) No association of the D4 gene with CD was found for the mothers. There was an association, however, for fathers.

For purpose of illustration, the fathers can be divided into delinquent and nondelinquent groups. The delinquent fathers were the top scorers on the CD scale ($N = 38$ men); the nondelinquents, the lower scores ($N = 79$ men). Of the 38 delinquent men, 18 (47 percent) carried the seven-repeat allele. Of the 79 nondelinquent men, 16 (20 percent) carried the predisposing allele. Thus, delinquent men were more likely than nondelinquent men to carry a seven-repeat allele.

A Serotonin Gene

In chapter 4 we saw that a higher level of blood platelet serotonin was associated with criminal behavior in Terrie Moffitt's study of young adults in New Zealand. A lower level of serotonin metabolites in the cerebral spinal fluid was found to be associated with violence and suicide. Thus, genes in the serotonin metabolic pathway may be related to criminal disposition. Some data are beginning to support this idea. Serotonin and dopamine seem to play some kind of balancing role in the nervous system. For example, in one mouse study, a gene in the dopamine pathway was completely eliminated—it was "knocked out"; the mice, because of the researcher's technological manipulations, were born without this gene (Gainetdinov et al. 1999). As a consequence, they were extremely hyperactive, but drugs that stimulated the serotonin metabolic pathways helped calm them down.

One interesting polymorphism resides in the HTR2A gene; this gene is a receptor for serotonin (Quist et al. 2000). This polymorphism is a SNP that changes the amino acid that is coded for: One allele codes for histidine, the other for tyrosine. The subjects were 143 children diagnosed with ADHD; they and their parents were genotyped. The tyrosine allele seemed to be causative of ADHD. It was transmitted to ADHD children 28 times and not transmitted 14 times, as against a chance expectation of 21 times each.

The MAOA Gene

This chapter opened with the example of the MAOA gene. The mutation found in the Dutch family is called a "null" mutation, because the gene fails to produce any functional MAOA protein. Another, more common polymorphism in the gene, called MAOA-uVNTR, may play a greater role in aggression and impulsivity. This polymorphism is a 30-base-pair repeat with two common alleles, A1 and A3, and two rare alleles, A2 and A4, that lie in a part of the gene called the promoter, which is found in the DNA sequence before the actual start of the MAOA gene's first coding region. The common alleles are one or two repeats long (i.e., 30 or 60 base pairs);

the uncommon ones, 1.5 and three repeats long. In the promoter region, repeats often regulate the rate at which a gene is copied into protein. Because the MAOA-uVNTR is on the X chromosome, men can carry only one allele; the gene does not exist on the Y chromosome.

In Manuck et al.'s (2000) study of antisocial traits, the subjects were men participating in a study of cholesterol at the University of Pittsburgh; they completed personality scales on aggression and impulsivity. Figure 5.3 presents a plot of the men's aggression/impulsivity scores by their genotypes. Considering just the two common alleles, the men who carried A1 had an aggression/impulsivity mean of 47.3, whereas those men who carried A3 had a mean of 51.7. This difference in trait mean levels is equivalent to a correlation coefficient of about .20 between the MAOA genotypes A1/A3 and aggression/impulsivity. In a blood test, the men who carried the protective allele A1 also had greater serotonin responsiveness—that is, a higher functioning serotoninogeric system that seemed to reduce their antisocial traits.

Figure 5.3

Association of Aggression Impulsivity and MAOA-uVNTR Alleles

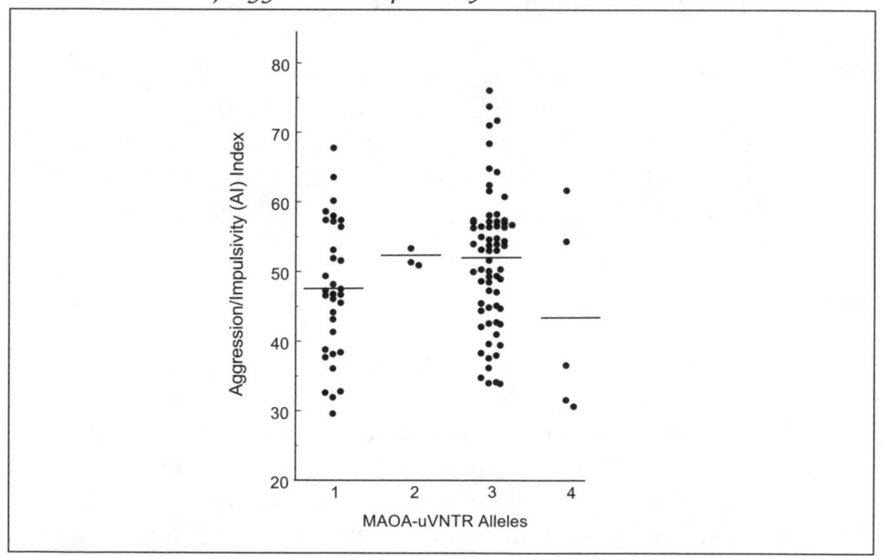

Source: Reprinted from Manuck, S. B., J. D. Flory, R. E. Ferrell, J. J. Mann, and M. F. Muldoon. 2000. "A Regulatory Polymorphism of the Monoamine Oxidase Gene-A May Be Associated With Variability in Aggression, Impulsivity, and Central Nervous System Serotonergic Responsivity." *Psychiatry Research* 95, 9–23. Copyright © Psychiatry Research. Reprinted with permission of Elsevier Science.

So, in returning to the MAOA gene, we now discover that it may indeed be a contributing cause to criminal disposition in the general population but that its effect strength is modest. Consider how the distributions of the men's scores overlap in Figure 5.3, with some individuals with A3 being less aggressive/impulsive than the men with the protective A1. The alleles involved in this polymorphism are also far more common than the rare allele that caused psychiatric disorder in the Dutch family.

Conclusion: From Genes to Criminal Disposition

The phrase a "gene for behavior" is really a metaphor. There are no genes for specific behaviors in humans; rather, the genes usually code for proteins, and the proteins in turn can affect and interact with a host of physiological systems. A gene that contributes to a behavioral trait, Alzheimer's disease, also contributes to a medical one, a higher risk of heart attacks. Among its many effects, a single gene may nudge a person toward a stronger criminal disposition. The more genes that nudge in this direction, the stronger the criminal disposition may become, up to some limit (Comings et al. 2000). The nudge from any single gene is not strong, and it could easily be countered by a favorable balance from another gene. We are at the dawn of learning about the genes that influence criminal disposition, a discovery process that will be slow and arduous. There is less to fear from these genes than many people would believe. In cases of in vitro fertilization, one could make a decision about which embryo to implant in a women's uterus on the basis of one gene, but probably not on the basis of a hundred or more genes. Perhaps a day will come when the strength of genetic dispositions can be predicted at birth, but it will not come soon. When, and if, it does come, let us hope that people have the wisdom to deal with that deeper knowledge of genetics and behavior.

Recommended Reading

Faraone, S. V., M. T. Tsuang, and D. W. Tsuang. 1999. *Genetics of Mental Disorders: A Guide for Students, Clinicians, and Researchers*. New York: Guilford Press. An easy-to-read introduction to psychiatric genetics with coverage of molecular genetic methods.

References

Blum, K., J. G. Cull, E. R. Braverman, and D. E. Comings. 1996. "Reward Deficiency Syndrome." *American Scientist* 84: 132–145.

Brunner, H. G., M. R. Nelen, X. O. Breakefield, H. H. Ropers, and B. A. van Oost. 1993. "Abnormal Behavior Associated With a Point Mutation in the Structural Gene for Monoamine Oxidase A. *Science* 262: 578–580.

Brunner, H. G., M. R. Nelen, P. van Zandvoort, N. G. Abeling, A. H. van Gennip, E. C. Wolters, M. A. Kulper, H. H. Ropers, and B. A. van Oost. 1991. "X-linked Borderline Mental Retardation With Prominent Behavioral Disturbance: Phenotype, Genetic Localization, and Evidence for Disturbed Monoamine Metabolism." *American Journal of Human Genetics* 52: 1032–1039.

Comings, D. E. 1998. "Polygenic Inheritance and Micro/Minisatellites." *Molecular Psychiatry* 3: 21–31.

Comings, D. E., R. Gade-Andavolu, N. Gonzalez, S. Wu, D. Muhleman, H. Blake, F. Chlu, E. Wang, K. Farwell, S. Darakjy, R. Baker, G. Dietz, G. Saucler, and P. MacMurray. 2000. "Multivariate Analysis of Associations of 42 Genes in ADHD, ODD and Conduct Disorder." *Clinical Genetics* 58: 31–40.

Ebstein, R. P., O. Novick, R. Umansky, B. Priel, Y. Osher, B. Blaine, E. R. Bennett, L. Nemanov, M. Katz, and R. H. Belmaker. 1996. "Dopamine D4 Receptor (D4DR) Exon III Polymorphism Associated With the Human Personality Trait of Novelty Seeking." *Nature Genetics* 12: 78–80.

Faraone, S. V., A. E. Doyle, E. Mick, and J. Diederman. 2001. "Meta-analysis of the Association Between the Dopamine D4 Gene seven-repeat Allele and Attention Deficit Hyperactivity Disorder." *American Journal of Psychiatry* 158: 1052–1057.

Faraone, S. V., M. T. Tsuang, and D. W. Tsuang. 1999. *Genetics of Mental Disorders: A Guide for Students, Clinicians, and Researchers.* New York: Guilford Press.

Gainetdinov, R. R., W. C. Wetsel, S. R. Jones, E. D. Levin, M. Jaber, and M. Caron. 1999. "Role of Serotonin in the Paradoxical Calming Effect of Psychostimulants on Hyperactivity." *Science* 283: 397–401.

Hamer, D. H., S. Hu, V. L. Magnuson, N. Hu, and A. M. L. Pattatucci. 1993. "A Linkage Between DNA Markers on the X Chromosome and Male Sexual Orientation." *Science* 261: 321–327.

Hamer, D. and L. Sirota. 2000. "Beware the Chopsticks Gene." *Molecular Psychiatry* 5: 11–13.

Lakatos, K., I. Toth, Z. Nemoda, K. Ney, M. Sasvari-Szekely, and J. Gervai. 2000. "Dopamine D4 Receptor (DRD4) Gene Polymorphism Is Associated With Attachment Disorganization in Infants." *Molecular Psychiatry* 5: 633–637.

Manuck, S. B., J. D. Flory, R. E. Ferrell, J. J. Mann, and M. F. Muldoon. 2000. "A Regulatory Polymorphism of the Monoamine Oxidase Gene-A May Be Associated With Variability in Aggression, Impulsivity, and Central Nervous System Serotoninergic Responsivity." *Psychiatry Research* 95: 9–23.

Ott, J. 1999. *Analysis of Genetic Linkage*, (3rd ed.). Baltimore: John Hopkins University Press.

Owen, M. J., A. G. Cardno, and M. C. O'Donovan. 2000. "Psychiatric Genetics: Back to the Future." *Molecular Psychiatry* 5: 22–31.

Plomin, R. 1994. "The Genetic Basis of Complex Human Behaviors." *Science* 264: 1733–1739.

Quist, J. F., C. L. Barr, R. Schachar, W. Roberts, M. Malone, R. Tannock, V. S. Basile, J. Beitchman, and J. L. Kennedy. 2000. "Evidence for the Serotonin HTR2A Receptor Gene as a Susceptibility Factor in Attention Deficit Hyperactivity Disorder (ADHD)." *Molecular Psychiatry* 5: 537–541.

Ridley, M. 1999. *Genome: The Autobiography of a Species in 23 Chapters*. New York: HarperCollins.

Rowe, D. C., C. Stever, D. Chase, S. Sherman, A. Abramowitz, and I. D. Waldman. 2001. "Two Dopamine Genes Related to Reports of Childhood Retrospective Inattention and Conduct Disorder." *Molecular Psychiatry* 6: 429–433.

Rowe, D. C., C. Stever, L. N. Giedinghagen, J. M. C. Gard, H. H. Cleveland, S. Terris, J. H. Mohr, S. Sherman, A. Abramowitz, and I. D. Waldman. 1998. "Dopamine DRD4 Receptor Polymorphism and Attention Deficit Hyperactivity Disorder." *Molecular Psychiatry* 3: 419–426.

Spielman, R. S. and W. J. Ewens. 1996. "The TDT and Other Family-based Tests for Linkage Disequilibrium and Association." *American Journal of Human Genetics* 59: 983–989.

Sunohara, G. A., W. Roberts, M. Malone, R. J. Schachar, R. Tannock, V. S. Basile, T. Wigal, S. B. Wigal, S. Schuck, J. Moriarty, J. M. Swanson, J. L. Kennedy, and C. L. Barr. 2000. "Linkage of the Dopamine D4 Receptor Gene and Attention-deficit/Hyperactivity Disorder." *Journal of the American Academy of Child and Adolescent Psychiatry* 39: 1537–1542. ✦

Chapter 6

Environmental Influences in Light of Genetic Findings

To a behavioral geneticist, the environment is everything that is not genetic. It encompasses everything from people talking to one another, to amniotic fluid that bathes a developing fetus. In this discipline, the environment encompasses TV ad jingles and lead poison in old paint. To most social scientists, the concept of environment is used more narrowly to mean the social environment of people's interactions with one another and their social circumstances. A sociologist might first mention socioeconomic status (SES) as a cause of crime—that is, whether children are born to parents who are rich or poor, well educated or unschooled. This discipline would be interested in the general characteristics of neighborhoods, as hinted at by whether store windows are barred and streets are lined with trash and graffiti, or store windows beautifully display merchandise along clean avenues. A psychologist might first emphasize intimacies of parent-child emotional bonds and parental discipline styles. Psychoanalysts would perhaps first mention emotional traumas from experiences during the first two years of life. The environment is such a broad concept that it is hard to know which environmental influence is most likely to be connected with crime.

An economist, Greg Duncan, and his colleagues have helped narrow the search for environmental influences on crime, at least in the late 1990s in the United States, with an analysis of which level of the environment makes adolescents alike in their crime rates (Duncan, Harris, and Boisjoly, in press). Their study included three kinds of kin: identical twins, fraternal twins, and full siblings, but it extended the analysis to environmental categories beyond sibling pairs. In particular, Duncan added best friends, neighbors, and classmates. The friends were of two types: mutual friends (Bill picks Harry, and Harry picks Bill in return) and unrequited friends (Bill picks Harry, but Harry picks someone else). In this study, each friend made his or her own self-report of delinquency.

The basic assumption of the study is that to the extent to which an environmental context determines delinquency rates, adolescents inhabiting that context should be alike. For example, if neighborhood is highly important, adolescents living in high-crime neighborhoods would tend to share a high crime rate, whereas adolescents living in a low-crime neighborhood would tend to share a low crime rate. Similarity of delinquency rates was assessed by a special kind of correlation coefficient that was equivalent for the different groups compared. In the case of neighborhood, a correlation of 0 would mean that adolescents living in the same census tract were unlike one another in their delinquency rates; a correlation of 1.0 would mean that they were perfectly alike.

Figure 6.1 displays Duncan's findings for each group. The siblings of all types were much alike in their delinquency rates. So were friends, whether best friends or unrequited friends. Because the choice of unrequited friends went in only one direction, it can be concluded that peers belonging to the same clique or crowd of friends were similar in their delinquency. Only slight similarity among individuals existed at the level of neighborhoods (i.e., census tracts) and classmates. Both environmental contexts were large enough to contain teenagers who were both highly delinquent and highly conforming.

The lack of neighborhood effects may seem surprising, given the emphasis on neighborhoods in anomie, strain, and several other criminological theories. One reason, as just stated, is that neighborhoods encompass larger populations, ensuring that people with different strengths of criminal disposition can be found within them. Children with strong risk factors for crime, such as poor parenting and hyperactivity, exhibit antisocial behaviors regardless of the economic level of their neighborhoods (Wikstrom and Loeber 2000). In Wikstrom and Loeber's study, economically disadvantaged public housing did "tip" boys with a weaker criminal disposition into crime; but these very worst neighborhoods were only a small proportion of all neighborhoods.

Figure 6.1

Similarity of Delinquency Rates for Various Classifications

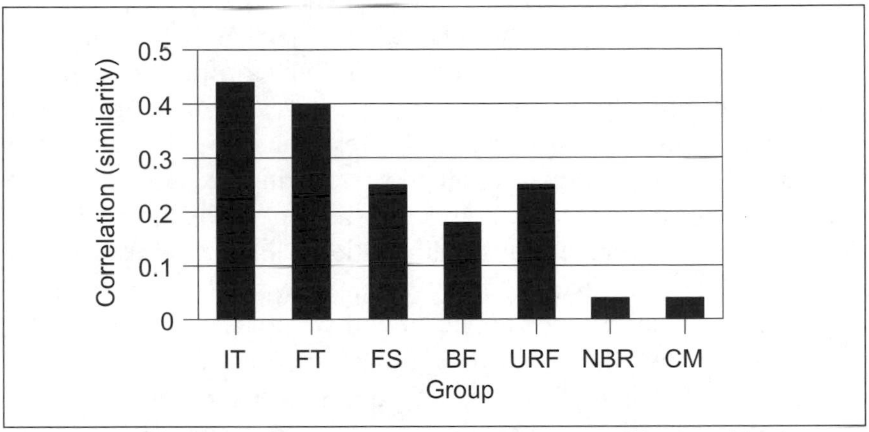

IT = identical twins; FT = fraternal twins; FS = full siblings; BF = best friends; URF = unrequited friends; NBR = neighborhood; CM = classmates.

Source: Data from Duncan, Harris, and Boisjoly. In press.

Wilkstrom and Loeber's finding reminded me of the one time my family was burglarized while I was a teenager. My mother was distraught because my grandfather's watch and other treasures were taken. The criminals had also left a calling card—they had defecated in the living room. Did these wanton criminal predators emerge under the cover of darkness from the worst borough of New York City to ransack my home on Long Island? No, when caught, the troubled teenage boys were living just a mile away from my home, in our middle-class neighborhood in a town known for its low crime rate and its small police booth. My mother's treasures were never recovered.

Social Class and Crime

Although sociologists and criminologists have devoted considerable effort to the relationship between socioeconomic status and crime, this association has received less attention from those interested in biology's relationship to crime. As shown by Duncan's findings, within any SES level people vary greatly in their criminality, so the overall association between SES and crime is a weak one. It is stronger for official crimes than for self-report crimes and for serious crimes than for trivial ones (Wolfgang, Thornberry, and Figlio 1987).

While some degree of association between SES and crime exists, its causal interpretation is problematic. First, social class is really a stand-in or proxy for some causal process that creates the SES-crime association. No one literally believes that parents' "seat time" in school somehow makes their children immune to influences that promote crime, although better-educated parents certainly accumulate more "seat time" than less-educated ones. Thus, social class itself is not very interesting unless a causal process linking it to crime is understood. Second, we can easily reverse the assumed direction of causation. To some degree, crime could produce a low SES; for example, periods of imprisonment interfere with employment, and many businesses refuse to accept a job applicant with a prior felony conviction.

Indeed, rather than viewing social class as a cause, a common approach in behavioral genetics is to consider another question, "What causes parental social class status?" This topic is beyond the scope of this book, but briefly, the argument is that (1) heritable traits partly determine the SES level achieved by adults, and (2) those heritable traits may partly determine criminal disposition and put offspring at risk, because genes favorable to crime may be inherited. Although there is not much evidence along these lines for most traits, we can speculate on how this might work. For example, a high activity level could aid a person in achieving a higher social status but at the same time put his child at risk for crime as part of a syndrome of hyperactivity. In this case, a heritable trait tends to dilute the SES-crime association, making it weaker. Another trait, IQ (as measured by IQ test scores), tends to make people rise or fall in social class level (Rowe, Vesterdal, and Rodgers 1998). Consider two brothers. The one with the IQ higher than his father's tends to rise in SES; the one whose IQ is lower tends to fall in SES level (Waller 1971). As there is a modest negative association between IQ and delinquency (Hirschi and Hindelang 1977), the heritable trait of IQ tends to strengthen the SES-crime association in the expected direction (i.e., lower-SES people committing more crimes). From this discussion, it is apparent that SES is a complex variable, and not one that to my thinking reveals clearly how the environment might affect criminal disposition.

If Duncan's findings are correct, the environmental contexts on which to focus the greatest attention would be the peer group and the family. Crime is strongly aggregated within these levels of analysis. The next two sections of this chapter examine these contexts from a genetically informed perspective.

Peer Groups, Gangs, and Crime

"When you're a Jet, you're always a Jet," shout the chorus in *West Side Story,* a musical about gangs in conflict loosely based on Shakespeare's play *Romeo and Juliet.* Conflict between the gangs leads tragically to the loss of an innocent woman's life and to the end of a first love affair, the lovers being divided by their gang loyalties. Simple statistics show that most delinquent acts are committed by small groups of boys. Adult criminals become more likely to commit crimes alone, but small groups are also common. Delinquent peer groups do not always have a conscious self-identity, marked by clothing, tattoos, graffiti, and other signs, like the "street gangs" most associated with disadvantaged inner-city neighborhoods. However, the self-conscious street gang does seem like a natural extension of the group nature of much delinquent activity. On the University of Arizona campus—where I teach—fraternity boys took to beating up men from other fraternities. Some 20 or more frat boys would attack a single, isolated victim—not a crime of great courage! In the 1990s on the Navajo reservation in northern Arizona, young Navajo men adopted the gang colors and dress of the Crips and Bloods of inner-city Los Angeles. Despite a great cultural distance from African Americans living in Los Angeles to Native Americans living in rural Arizona, the attraction of the gang was strong; violent and antisocial groups of adolescents boys appear to be a social universal.

The importance of friends in Duncan's research data appears in the ~.25 correlation between friends' delinquency. Yet the social scientist recognizes immediately that this association presents a problem for causal interpretation. Friends may be alike in their delinquency rates because "birds of a feather flock together"—that is, adolescents with similar levels of criminal disposition manage to befriend one another. This pathway of causation certainly seems more plausible than the other extreme—an evil delinquent boy befriending a timid computer geek and somehow transforming him into a menace to the community. On the other hand, the association could come from influence as well. One can easily imagine boys daring a friend to try something illegal, and a relatively well-behaved boy yielding to their pressure. Yet another pathway of influence would be two boys with criminal dispositions egging each other on and committing a greater number of delinquent acts than either boy would on his own. Thus, the most likely *a priori* interpretation is that the .25 association is the result of a mixture of selection and influence processes. To see the full .25 association as friends causing misbehavior would certainly overestimate the power of friends; yet the opposite extreme is probably equally wrong. While this interpretation is intuitively appealing, proving it to the satisfaction of the social scientist is actually difficult, because we cannot control individuals' friendship choices.

Ironically, suitable evidence for a causal influence of peers has been provided by a well-intentioned social intervention that failed. In the Adolescent Transitions Program (Dishion, McCord, and Poulin 1999), high-risk boys and girls were randomly assigned to a treatment condition called "teen focus groups," in which the teenagers met in small groups to discuss earning a high school degree and controlling their anger. Unhappily, the focus group adolescents did worse on a three-year outcome evaluation than a control group did. According to teachers who were unaware of the treatment conditions, the teen focus participants had higher levels of delinquent behavior than the controls over the three-year follow-up period, an effect that was strongest for the older participants. Dishion believes that the flaw of the teen focus program was that it brought high-risk boys together, giving them the opportunity to form friendships and to encourage one another's penchant for delinquent behavior.

In a related study, Dishion made videotapes of high-risk boys talking to each other in pairs. He discovered that the more antisocial boys tended to reward each other's talk of breaking the law with laughter or other positive responses. Boys whose friendship was characterized by this kind of mutual encouragement were more likely to show an increase in their self-reported delinquency within a year or two than were boys whose talk was more conventional. Because the Adolescent Transitions Program was an experimental design, we can be more confident that the boys' delinquency was increased by friends' influence. The study also teaches another lesson: Don't assume that because a social invention sounds good in theory that it cannot be harmful.

There is ample evidence for the other type of process of friends' shared criminality: selection. One of the strongest pieces of evidence for a selection process is that criminal disposition may exist before friendships develop in adolescence. In one long-term study of children all born in one year (a birth cohort), three-year-old children were distinguished according to whether they had temper tantrums (Caspi 2000). Anger and temper in the three-year-old children predicted their criminal behavior, antisocial personality disorder, suicide attempts, and alcohol dependence at 21 years. Unless we invoke time travel, hanging out with bad peer company did not provoke the three-year-olds to their temper tantrums. Vitaro et al. (1997) found that only adolescents with moderately strong predispositions toward antisocial behavior were most influenced by friends' aggressiveness; highly disruptive and highly conforming boys were the least influenced.

Another research design in which a selection process can be revealed is to watch friendships form and dissolve. In 1978, Kandel completed a classic study by following friendship formation and dissolution during a school year. Her study focused on four characteristics, including minor delinquency. Her finding was that before forming a friendship during the school year, prospective friends were already similar to each other in their levels of minor delinquency. On minor delinquency, the correlation of "friends to be" at the start of the school year was .25. The correlation on delinquency of friends who remained friends throughout the school year was .29. Thus, to count the full .29 correlation as entirely "influence" would be to misinterpret its origin, because some part of the .29 association existed before friendship formation (i.e., a selection process). Kandel also found that friendships that dissolved during the school year tended to be those between the most behaviorally dissimilar friends. She also observed a second phenomenon, friends becoming more similar during the duration of their friendships. Using a complex statistical test, Kandel determined that about half of friends' similarity was due to selection and half to influence (Kandel 1978, 1996).

The role of friends in delinquency has led to a comparison of delinquency to a contagious viral or bacterial disease. Crime, most certainly, is not an epidemic disease; the use of the concept is meant only as an analogy. Crime is like an epidemic in that it "spreads" in face-to-face encounters among people. What is transmitted is not a disease organism, but some psychological encouragement to commit criminal acts and to notice the opportunities to do so. Like a flu epidemic sweeping through a community, crime is "caught" by ever greater numbers of adolescents, particularly those who will desist from criminal acts by young adulthood (see Moffit, in chapter 2). If one follows a birth cohort through their teenage years, at first, in the early teens, the number who are arrested grows slowly; by age 13 to 16, the increase is most rapid, and then at ages 16 and greater, fewer and fewer are added to the group of arrested teenagers. Mathematically, this growth curve fits closely to an epidemic's growth curve (Jones 1998), which is also found with other behaviors that spread during adolescence, such as cigarette smoking (Rowe, Rodgers, and Gilson 2000).

This analogy has its limitations, of course. Susceptibility to a disease does not change much during adolescence, and the main culprit is exposure to the virus or bacterium. Adolescents may be more prone to crime as a consequence of pubertal development (Flannery, Rowe, and Gulley 1993), so their "susceptibility" to a friend's encouragement of crime does change during these years. And, of course, no one goes looking to catch a virus, but some violent adolescents do go "looking" for a fight. Nonetheless, the broad fit of epidemic spread to crime in adolescents again emphasizes the influence of peers in its genesis.

Table 6.1
Sibling Resemblance (Correlation) by Mutual Friendship Category

Group	Delinquency *r*	Substance Use *r*
Brothers		
Separate friends	.20	.22
Mutual friends	.63	.66
Sisters		
Separate friends	.33	.29
Mutual friends	.65	.84

Sample sizes range from 18 sibling pairs to 124 pairs. Substance use included drinking alcoholic beverages, smoking cigarettes or marijuana, and using inhalants.

Friends' and siblings' mutual influence can also change the degree to which siblings resemble each other (Carey 1992; Rowe and Gulley

1992). In a study of young adolescents (mean age 13.5 years) in Tucson, Arizona, I compared the behavioral resemblance of siblings who had many mutual friends (about 20 percent of brothers and 13 percent of sisters) with those who had fewer mutual friends. These data are summarized in Table 6.1. Sibling resemblances for rates of substance use and delinquency were much greater for siblings who reported spending a great deal of time with mutual friends versus those who did not. One way to misinterpret this finding is to think that having mutual friends made an adolescent more delinquent. This interpretation was false; siblings with mutual friends were not any more delinquent, on average, than those without them. What differentiated the two groups was how much siblings resembled each other. Consider a pair of siblings who spend time with mutual friends who are delinquent; they are both exposed to any encouragement of antisocial behavior coming from these friends. At the other extreme, consider two siblings who hang out with fellow members of the chess and physics clubs. Their mutual friendship probably discourages delinquency. Thus, friends' influence makes sibling pairs alike, sometimes making a pair more delinquent, sometimes making one more conformist, so that overall no relationship would exist between sharing friends and the level of substance use or delinquency. Another lesson of my finding is that siblings' behavioral resemblance is not always a genetic or family environmental effect. Controlling statistically for parental discipline styles did not change the increase in siblings behavioral resemblance caused by having mutual friends.

Behavioral geneticists have a term for environmental influences that can operate to magnify genetic predispositions: the *genotype-environment correlation*. Genotype and environment are correlated because particular genotypes are more likely to wind up in particular environments than chance alone would allow. Height gives a genetic advantage to a basketball player, and taller people are more likely than short ones to be found on high school basketball courts. Tallness alone does not make one a good basketball player, but it does provide encouragement for trying out for a basketball team, and a taller child may catch the coach's eye. For height and basketball playing, a modest correlation between genotype (i.e., those genes that make a child short or tall) and environment (i.e., the opportunities to play basketball) would exist. Those tall children who learn to play well increase the genotype-environment correlation for basketball by encouraging coaches and players to pay more attention to tall children as potential recruits.

Similarly, inheritance of a criminal disposition is correlated with crime-reinforcing environments in the form of "bad apple" peers. Crime rates could probably be reduced if adolescents with criminal friends were forced to join the chess and science clubs and seek their friendships within those groups, but I doubt that any such effort is practical. A lesson of Dishion's experimental study is that we should avoid bringing youths with criminal dispositions together, at least when feasible at the institutional level, a warning captured in the cliché that "prisons are schools for crime." In behavioral genetics, another phrase that catches this indirect route of genetic influence is *nature via nurture.* Although the genes that influence eye color would not require a specific form of environmental help, those that influence a complex behavioral characteristic such as crime certainly do need the social environment to perform some of the "heavy lifting."

Genotype X Environment Interactions

Another way in which the environment may influence crime is through a genotype x environment interaction. Technically, a genotype x environment interaction occurs when the developmental response of a genotype depends on a particular environmental condition, and it can vary widely across environments. An example is obesity in the Pima Indians of the Southwest. These Native Americans have a life expectancy of only 54 years because of their high prevalence of obesity and of a medical complication often associated with it, diabetes. The Pima Indians have chosen to consume an American-style high-fat diet and are relatively sedentary, unlike members of the same tribe living today in Mexico just south of the Arizona border. The Mexican branch of the Pima tribe has a more traditional diet and engages in more physical activity. These Indians have remained of normal weight and have kept a low rate of diabetes. We presume that the genotypes of the two groups are fairly similar; indeed, their tribal boundaries do criss-cross the Mexico-United States border. They differ because the same genotype has responded dramatically to lifestyle changes.

One explanation for this effect is the existence of "thrifty" genes that may protect the body against caloric loss during famine. If Pima

Indians possess these protective genes, they may be more susceptible to gaining weight when food is abundant. Another population showing this same pattern of weight change on exposure to a Western diet are the Samoan people of the West Samao Islands.

We can postulate a genotype x environment interaction for crime in that children who inherit a criminal disposition may be more sensitive than other children to adverse family circumstances. Child abuse is statistically associated with aggression and violence (Dodge, Bates, and Petitt 1990), and case histories exist of criminals who have endured a terribly abusive upbringing. Albert DeSalvo, infamously known as the Boston Strangler, was raised by an abusive father who beat one son until he was a mass of visible bruises and once punished his wife by methodically breaking every one of her fingers (Everitt 1999). Yet Albert DeSalvo was one of six children, all of whom had extensive exposure to their dysfunctional parents. Only he went on to commit multiple rapes and the brutal murders of women. Because siblings each must differ in their genetic dispositions, it may be that DeSalvo was the only affected child because of his particularly predisposing genes, ones not shared by his siblings. Of course, we cannot prove that this is true of Albert DeSalvo, even if a genetic test were available; in 1973 he was stabbed to death by another prison inmate. However, we can find less dramatic but more compelling data on genotype x environment interaction in an adoption study by the psychiatrist Remi Cadoret and his colleagues (1995).

Cadoret used a design that "looked back" at the biological parents of adopted-away children to determine the children's predispositions. If the biological parents had a criminal or alcohol abuse history, their child was classified as predisposed toward aggression. If the parents were free of psychiatric disorders, the child was classified in the control group. This method of classification does not imply that all the at-risk children carried some genetic criminal disposition; just as brown-eyed parents can have a blue-eyed child, not every child would inherit criminally predisposing genes from his or her parents. Nonetheless, on average, criminal dispositions should be more common among the adoptive children with biological parents who carried a psychiatric diagnosis than in the control children.

All the adoptive children had been separated from their biological parents at birth and placed with an adoptive family—the family that constituted their upbringing environment. An environmental risk score was created from a count of problems that existed in the adoptive families; that is, adoptive parents who were divorced, who were separated, or had various psychiatric disorders had a greater risk than those adoptive parents with fewer problems. As adolescents, the adoptees who had both the biological criminal disposition and an adverse adoptive family environment had the greatest number of aggressive symptoms. To state this another way, the relationship between family-environmental risk and aggression was stronger in criminally predisposed adoptees than in the control adoptees. Figure 6.2 presents these data, showing one line for the predisposed and another for the control adoptive children, who were adolescents when interviewed.

Figure 6.2

Interaction Between Adoptive Children's Genetic Disposition and Adoptive Family

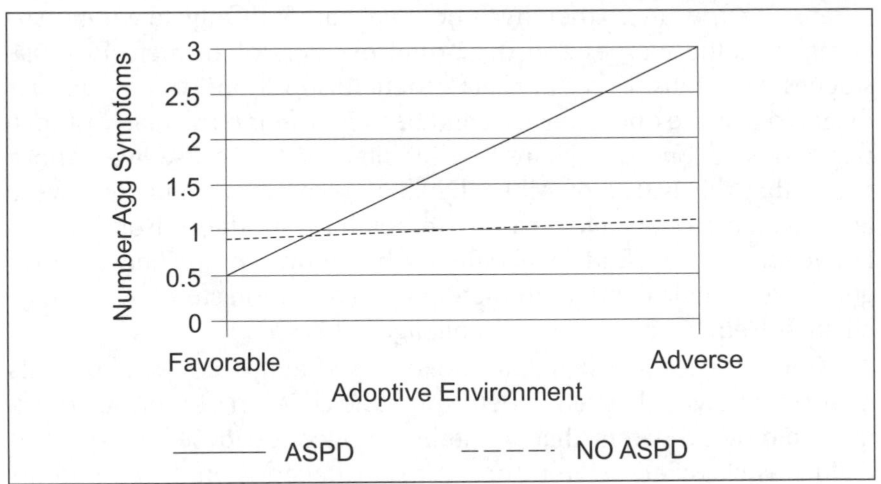

ASPD = Antisocial personality disorder in adoptive child's biological parents; Agg. = aggressivity.

Source: Adapted from Cadoret, R. J., W. R. Yates, E. Troughton, G. Woodworth, and M. A. Stewart. 1995. "Genetic-environmental Interaction in the Genesis of Aggressivity and Conduct Disorders." *Archives of General Psychiatry* 52, 916–924. Copyright © American Medical Association. Adapted with permission.

These family circumstances were not nearly as bad as DeSalvo's, but they appeared to particularly influence children with some genetic criminal disposition. One could argue for a reverse causality, however. For example, perhaps an acting-out child drove the adoptive parents to divorce–an idea that may seem ridiculous until one witnesses the great difficulty of raising an antisocial child. Cadoret examined this possibility and found that it could not account for the findings. However, other studies have established that criminal disposition in an adoptive child can affect the parenting style of the adoptive parents (for details, see Ge et al. 1996).

Raine and his colleagues (1998) have produced persuasive data on environmental effects at the level of brain physiology. His subjects were 41 people tried for murder or attempted murder in California compared with 41 age- and sex-matched controls. The murderers were further subdivided into those from deprived childhood backgrounds and those from more ordinary backgrounds. An example of a deprived background would be repeated physical or sexual abuse in childhood. Brain sugar metabolism was measured on both the murderers and controls using a PET scan (see chapter 4 for a description of PET scanning). In the controls, the cortex behind the forehead lit up on the PET scan, showing a rapid metabolism of sugar; their brain cells were sucking up sugar fuel. The brains of the deprived murderers looked much the same. Their medial prefrontal cortex lit up as well. In contrast, the nondeprived murderers had an abnormal pattern of brain metabolism, utilizing less sugar in their prefrontal cortex area than either the deprived murderers or the controls. This pattern of nervous system underarousal characterized only the nondeprived murderers. Raine's interpretation was that deprived murderers were more compelled to their crime by their environmental histories and hence were more neurologically normal. He did not, however, find the group of murderers that we might expect from Cadoret's study: those with abnormal brain physiology whose murderous tendencies were augmented by an adverse environment. Perhaps this missing group would be found in a PET scan study of a greater number of murderers.

Historical Changes in Crime Rates

Crime rates change through historical periods; they go up, and they go down. Large riots occurred in Philadelphia in the 1830s and 1840s. Youth gangs formed around Irish and German immigrant workers and split along religious lines: Catholic versus Protestant. Whites clashed with African Americans. Policing could not keep pace with the high frequency of violent and nonviolent crimes. Ours is not the first era to experience high rates of violence, and certainly cities in the United States are far safer places today than they were in that antebellum period. In the Prohibition era of the 1920s, social drinkers became criminals with the outlawing of alcoholic beverages, and criminal gangs fought to control the distribution of alcohol, much as urban gangs have fought over the control of drugs such as cocaine, heroin, and marijuana in recent decades. From 1973 to 1993, the rate of violent crime in the FBI's Uniform Crime Report about doubled (Lykken 1997). However, violent crime rates have been declining since the early 1990s, with the most recent data showing a decrease in the rate of decline.

Rates of historical change certainly outpace those of genetic change in a population. I do not mean that the genetic composition of a population is static. It is never so; natural selection and other processes are constantly changing gene frequencies for particular alleles (i.e., variants of a particular gene, see chapter 5). However, changes in prevalence of criminal disposition attributable to genes in a population are likely to be slower than changes in crime rates, especially rates of specific crimes. In the case of Prohibition, a new crime—drinking alcoholic beverages—was created by the stroke of a pen that signed a bill into law. Genetic dispositions to become addicted to alcohol could not, and did not, change more than slightly in the same year. Indeed, it makes sense to divide the historical change questions into two separate questions: (1) How do historical changes in society affect the rates of crime, even without altering the prevalence of criminal disposition? (2) How does history change the prevalence (i.e., the percentage affected in a population) of people with a criminal disposition?

Changing Crime Rates Without Affecting the Root Causes of Crime

How could environments affect crime without affecting criminal dispositions? One way is by imprisoning people or by releasing them. Fidel Castro managed to cause a minicrime wave when he released large numbers of men from Cuban prisons and allowed them to resettle in the United States. Many of these Mariel boat-lift men were quickly back in jail, for crimes they committed in this country. Some scholars believe that the currently high rate of imprisonment in the United States has reduced our overall crime rate. Assuredly, a policy of greater imprisonment does little to change the number of people with a criminal disposition; it just moves them between places—residing in prison versus living free in society.

Another form of deterrence against crime results from the "broken windows" theory first advanced by James Q. Wilson and George L. Kelling in an article in the *Atlantic Monthly* (Miller 2001). Their idea was that an unrepaired broken window signals would-be criminals that no effective policing exists in a community; in effect, the physical breakdown and disorganization of a community may tell criminals that committing crime carries few costs. Wilson and Kelling advocated focusing police efforts on reducing signs of neighborhood disorganization, such as graffiti, litter, neglected buildings, and minor criminal misconduct.

Their advice was taken to heart by the chief of the New York City Transit Police, William Bratton. He enforced laws against minor crimes, such as jumping turnstiles in the subway to avoid paying fares. By enforcing the law against turnstile jumping, the transit police managed to catch more serious perpetrators as well, including young men carrying guns or with outstanding arrest warrants against them. Crime rates in the New York subway system dropped dramatically. When Bratton later became the citywide police commissioner, he extended the "broken windows" policies to the whole city. Among other changes, he eliminated the "squeegee men" who cleaned car windows on crowded city streets.

When my father and I drove from Long Island into New York City, we entered Manhattan through the Lincoln Tunnel. I recall the intimidating squeegee men who, muscled and tattooed, made no announcement before spraying our car window and starting to clean it. Caught in bumper-to-bumper New York traffic, you could not escape them. I was glad to see them go. Bratton's new policies also eliminated or reduced many other minor violations of the criminal codes in New York, and crime rates across New York City fell, as they did in the nation as a whole during this period in the 1990s.

A spate of recent books and articles have been critical of the crime reduction claimed by the broken-window-policies advocates (Harcourt 2001; Karmen 2001; Sampson 1999; but see Kelling and Coles 1998). Their arguments illustrate the difficulty of tying historical change to any particular environmental event. Many changes occur at once in society, so how can one tease them apart? Miller (2001) mentions just a few of the "possible suspects" for the change in crime rates:

> One way of interpreting the evidence of the 1990s . . . is the reverse of Murphy's Law: Virtually everything that could go right, did. Turf wars in the crack trade died down. The number of young males between the ages of 18 and 24—the crime-prone years—shrank. Unbroken economic growth provided disadvantaged young people with attractive alternatives to crime. In addition, scholars credit public policies, such as those that led to higher rates of incarceration. (A16)

Other critics correctly charge that studies of the broken windows policy have not had good control groups or have not included neighborhoods in which the policies were not adopted. Equivalent control groups are needed to prove the counterfactual—i.e., that in the absence of the broken windows policy, crime rates would have remained high.

My own view is that the broken windows policy and other forms of more effective policing did contribute to the reduction in crime. I do not have hard scientific evidence to back up my view; it may partly reflect my pleasure on seeing the squeegee men disappear. However, at least the timing was right; a change in police practices, in many jurisdictions, did coincide with crime-rate reductions. As the critics believe, I too doubt that changes in police policies were the *full* explanation for the crime reduction in the 1990s. To untangle the causes, we will need further changes in crime rates, and studies must be designed to catch neighborhoods as they undergo transitions from high to low crime rates—or, unfortunately as is likely in the future because of an increasing proportion of adolescents in the U.S. population, the opposite.

Changing Crime Rates by Affecting the Root Causes of Crime

We have developed a short list of causal influences on crime: peer influence and genotype x environment interactions during childhood. Of the two, the best candidate for affecting the prevalence of criminal dispositions is formative family influences, both genetic and environmental, on behavioral development. The peer influences may activate more than create a criminal disposition in adolescence. Could changes in the family have historically altered the prevalence of criminal dispositions? In thinking about this process, for convenience I'm treating criminal dispositions as categorical rather than continuous. Could in one generation three men out of 100 men possess a criminal disposition while in another, five men in 100?

Changes in criminal disposition have not been tracked historically because no simple measurement exists for its presence or absence. The rates of criminal disposition need not track crime rates precisely. Indeed, imprisonment, more effective policing, and the end of a drug use epidemic could reduce crime rates while deeper historical forces increase the prevalence of criminal disposition, creating a possibility of a rapid growth in crime rates if social conditions became more favorable. Indeed, the distinction between criminal disposition and crime rates is like that between genotype and phenotype in behavioral genetics. The "phenotype" consists of countable criminal acts such as burglaries and assaults; they are the surface manifestation of a criminal disposition. The disposition itself consists of biological characteristics, which may be induced both genetically and environmentally, that contribute to the likelihood of committing criminal acts. Thus, in a given generation, more people might be born with less volume in the frontal cortex and with a low resting heart rate, two of Raine's biological markers of criminal disposition, during a period of declining crime rates.

Figure 6.3

Relative Curves for the Violent Crime-Rate, Population Composition, and Lagged Fatherless Rearing (15 Years Prior Illegitimacy and Divorce Rates, Combined)

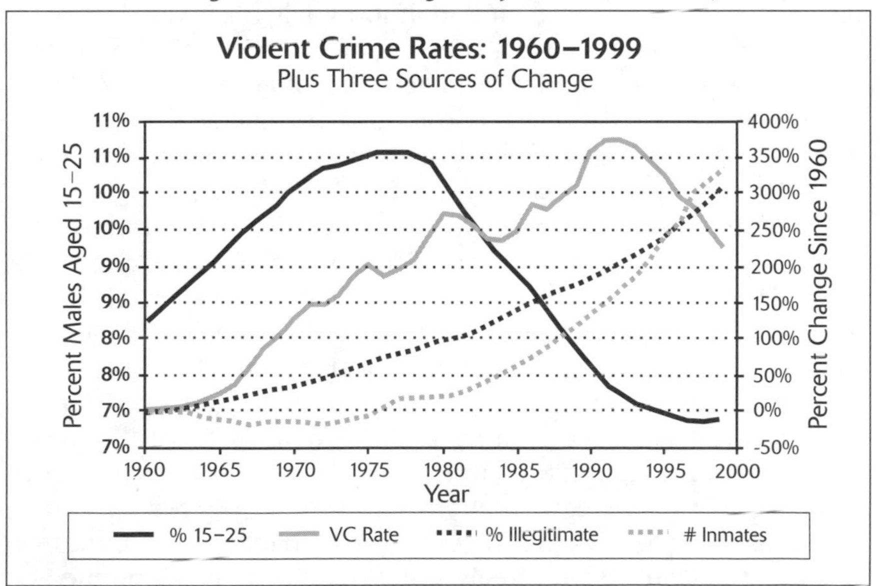

Source: Lykken, D. T. 2001, August. "Parental Licensure." Presentation at the American Psychological Association Meeting, San Francisco, CA.

However, lacking any other proxy, crime rates have been used to index changes in the frequency of criminal disposition. Lykken (1995, personal communication) has analyzed the changes in the rate of aggravated assaults between the years 1960 and 1999. The violent crime rate was almost four times greater in the early 1990s than it was in 1960. Since the 1990s, the violent crime rate has dropped, but it is still about 2.5 times greater than it was in 1960.

As shown in Figure 6.3, Lykken's model of violent crime contains three main predictors. One is the percentage change in the number of inmates; he reasoned that removing criminals from the street can reduce crime rates. His second variable is the lagged percentage of illegitimate births; this variable correlates closely with the number of children raised in single-parent households. Lykken identified rearing in single-parent households as particularly important for crime because children of single mothers were seven times more likely to be convicted of a violent crime than the children of two parents. Thus, relatively small increases in the rate of single-parent families should translate into a disproportionate increase in the overall violent crime rate. The effect of single-parent households on children's crime risk might also represent a Cadoret-style genotype x environment interaction, with genetically disposed children reared in single-parent households developing an even stronger criminal disposition, which is then played out in adolescence and adulthood. His third variable was a population composition, i.e., the percentage of the males aged 15 to 25, the age group responsible for about half of all crimes of violence. By combining population composition, percentage of illegitimacy, and number of inmates, Lykken's model can accurately track the changing rates of violent crime from 1960 to 1999.

Is Lykken's model correct? We cannot say for sure. Although the influences he pinpointed were associated with the violent crime rate, other models can be constructed to account for this historical change. For example, instead of being increased by single-parent families, the crime rate in the early 1980s may have been boosted by the epidemic of crack smoking and the harsh prosecution of drug users and dealers, that occurred during the same period. In accord with Lykken's emphasis on the illegitimacy rate, a controversial theory has been advanced that an increase in abortions in the 1970s reduced crime rates years later because fewer "unwanted" children were born than would have been without freely available abortions (Donohue and Levitt in press). The historical study of change in crime rates is frustrating because there are clues to the existence of big environmental variables, powerful ones with large effects, but against the constantly changing flux of the economy, social mores, public policy changes, and policing practices, they may be hard to isolate and understand.

Conclusions

The existence of a modest genetic influence on variation in criminal disposition is perfectly consistent with a simultaneous influence of the social environment. Friends' influence is one motivator for increased criminal behavior among genetically disposed individuals, and probably for increased conformity in those individuals possessing an opposing genetic disposition. Although peer groups can foster criminal activity, they are also difficult for policymakers to change, because in the United States people possess a constitutionally protected freedom to choose anyone as friends and to assemble in public. Adverse family environments also appear to strengthen the likelihood of aggression and other antisocial behaviors, especially in those individuals who are genetically predisposed. Interventions can be directed at parental behavior, although changing parental behavior is not easy, and the least capable parents are the ones who are most difficult to retain in an intervention program. Public policies that focus on imprisonment and on the quality of life in neighborhoods can also successfully reduce crime rates. Such approaches, however, are mired in a deeper political argument about which kinds of freedoms must be sacrificed or limited to achieve crime reduction. The broken windows approach may be accompanied by increased random stopping of people based on their physical appearance and may disproportionately target ethnic minorities (racial profiling). Thus, these policies may be opposed by political liberals, regardless of whether they successfully reduce crime rates.

Historical changes in crime rates have been large and point to the existence of powerful environmental levers to reduce crime. The cause of a historical change, however, is also most resistant to analysis and replication, so an understanding of why crime rates fall and rise continues as a source of controversy among scholars. It is well to remember that the causes of America's Great Depression are still debated, some 70 years after the event. I have not covered a large research literature on interventions programs to reduce crime, some of which have produced a limited success (e.g., Tremblay et al. 1995). In summary, the existence of some genetic influence on criminal disposition should not discourage partial and true experimental studies of ways in which to reduce crime via policy changes and targeted social interventions. It is unwise either to promise too much or not to try at all.

Recommended Reading

Lykken, D. T. 1995. *The Antisocial Personalities.* Hillsdale, NJ: Lawrence Erlbaum. This book explores explanations of the historical change in crime rates and places more emphasis on the influence of the family than I have done in this book. Lykken illustrates the diversity of views among biologically oriented theories of crime.

References

Cadoret, R. J., W. R. Yates, E. Troughton, G. Woodworth, and M. A. Stewart. 1995. "Genetic-environmental Interaction in the Genesis of Aggressivity and Conduct Disorders." *Archives of General Psychiatry* 52: 916–924.

Carey, G. 1992. "Twin Imitation for Antisocial Behavior: Implications for Genetic and Family Research." *Journal of Abnormal Psychology* 101: 18–25.

Caspi, A. 2000. "The Child Is Father of the Man: Personality Continuities From Childhood to Adulthood." *Journal of Personality and Social Psychology* 78: 158–172.

Dishion, T. J., J. McCord, and F. Poulin. 1999. "When Interventions Harm: Peer Groups and Problem Behavior." *American Psychologist* 54: 755–764.

Dodge, K. A., J. E. Bates, and G. S. Pettit. 1990. "Mechanisms in the Cycle of Violence." *Science* 250: 1678–1683.

Donohue, J. J. III, and S. D. Levitt. In press. "The Impact of Legalizing Abortion on Crime." *Quarterly Journal of Economics.*

Duncan, G. J., K. M. Harris, and J. Boisjoly. In press. "Sibling, Peer, Neighbor, and Schoolmate Correlations as Indicators of the Importance of Context for Adolescent Development." *Demography.*

Everitt, D. 1999. "Desalvo, Albert (1931–1973)." In R. Gottesman and R. M. Brown (eds.), *Violence in America: An Encyclopedia*, pp. 393–394. New York: Charles Scribner's Sons.

Flannery, D. J., D. C. Rowe, and B. L. Gulley. 1993. "Impact of Pubertal Status, Timing, and Age on Adolescent Sexual Experience and Delinquency." *Journal of Adolescent Research* 8: 21–40.

Ge, X., R. D. Conger, R. J. Cadoret, J. M. Neiderhiser, W. Yates, E. Troughton, and M. A. Stewart. 1996. "The Developmental Interface Between Nature and Nurture: A Mutual Influence Model of Child Antisocial Behavior and Parent Behaviors." *Developmental Psychology* 32: 574–589.

Harcourt, B. E. 2001. *Illusion of Order: The False Promise of Broken Windows*. Cambridge, MA: Harvard University Press.

Hirschi, T. and M. J. Hindelang. 1977. "Intelligence and Delinquency: A Revisionist Review." *American Sociological Review* 42: 571–587.

Jones, M. B. 1998. "Behavioral Contagion and Official Delinquency: Epidemic Course in Adolescence." *Social Biology* 45: 134–142.

Kandel, D. B. 1978. "Homophily, Selection and Socialization in Adolescent Friendships." *American Journal of Sociology* 84: 427–436.

—. 1996. "The Parental and Peer Context of Adolescent Deviance: An Algebra of Interpersonal Influences." *Journal of Drug Issues* 26: 289–315.

Karmen, A. 2001. *New York Murder Mystery: The True Story Behind the Crime Crash of the 1990s*. New York: New York University Press.

Kelling, G. L. and C. M. Coles. 1998. *Fixing Broken Windows: Restoring Order and Reducing Crime in Our Communities*. New York: Free Press.

Lykken, D. T. 1995. *The Antisocial Personalities*. Hillsdale, NJ: Lawrence Erlbaum Associates.

—. 1997. "The American Crime Factory." *Psychological Inquiry* 8: 261–270.

Miller, D. W. 2001. "Poking Holes in the Theory of 'Broken Windows'." *The Chronicle of Higher Education* 47: Feb. 9, A14–A16.

Raine, A., J. Stoddard, S. Bihrle, and M. Buchsbaum. 1998. "Prefrontal Glucose Deficits in Murderers Lacking Psychosocial Deprivation." *Neuropsychiatry, Neuropsychology, and Behavioral Neurology* 11: 1–7.

Rowe, D. C. and B. L. Gulley. 1992. "Sibling Effects on Substance Use and Delinquency." *Criminology* 30: 217–233.

Rowe, D. C., J. L. Rodgers, and M. Gilson. 2000. "Epidemics of Smoking: Modeling Tobacco Use Among Adolescents." In J. S. Rose, L. Chassin, C. C. Presson, and S. J. Sherman (eds.), *Multivariate Applications in Substance Use Research*, pp. 233–258. New York: Lawrence Erlbaum.

Rowe, D. C., W. J. Vesterdal, and J. L. Rodgers. 1998. "Herrnstein's Syllogism: Genetic and Shared Environmental Influences on IQ, Education, and Income. *Intelligence* 26: 405–423.

Sampson, R. J. 1999. "Systematic Social Observation of Public Spaces: A New Look at Disorder in Urban Neighborhoods." *American Journal of Sociology* 105: 603–651.

Tremblay, R. E., L. Pagani-Kurtz, L. C. Masse, and F. Viaro. 1995. "A Bimodal Preventive Intervention for Disruptive Kindergarten Boys: Its Impact Through Midadolescence." *Journal of Consulting and Clinical Psychology* 63: 560–568.

Vitaro, F., R. E. Tremblay, M. Kerr, L. Pagani, and W. M. Bukowski. 1997. "Disruptiveness, Friends' Characteristics, and Delinquency in Early Adolescence: A Test of Two Competing Models of Development." *Child Development* 68: 676–689.

Waller, J. H. 1971. "Achievement and Social Mobility: Relationships Among IQ Score, Education, and Occupation in Two Generations." *Social Biology* 18: 252–259.

Wikstrom, P. H. and R. Loeber. 2000. "Do Disadvantaged Neighborhoods Cause Well-adjusted Children to Become Adolescent Delinquents? A Study of Male Juvenile Serious Offending, Individual Risk and Protective Factors, and Neighborhood Context." *Criminology* 38: 1109–1142.

Wolfgang, M. E., T. P. Thornberry, and R. M. Figlio. 1987. *From Boy to Man, From Delinquency to Crime.* Chicago: University of Chicago Press. ✦

Chapter 7

A Look Ahead: Implications for Criminal Justice Policy and Ethical Concerns

Bill Morrill had uncontrollable sexual urges (Slater 2000). Although married, he cruised for hours to pick up prostitutes and had sex at every opportunity. His sexual urges became so uncontrolled that he contemplated suicide as a way out. Another man, Vince, became sexually aroused by women's clothing and crossed-dressed when his wife would not catch him. Both Morrill and Vince, along with other men showing abnormal sexual behavior, became patients of Dr. Martin Kafka, at McLean Hospital outside of Boston. Dr. Kafka treated them with the drug Prozac or one of its chemical relatives, all belonging to the class of drugs called serotonin reuptake inhibitors (SRIs). These drugs, which increase serotonin levels in the brain, are commonly used to treat major depression and obsessive-compulsive disorders. They also have a side effect that in most cases is highly undesirable: they reduce sexual drive. According to Kafka, many of his patients had greatly improved control over their sexual impulses once they began taking one of the SRI drugs. Morrill's sex drive was nearly eliminated; he reported that he had sex with his wife only when she insisted and that he could not maintain an erection very long. Vince had a better clinical outcome; his desire to cross-dress was removed and his sexual relations with his wife remained normal. The newspaper article describing Kafka's therapy, however, fails to present overall statistics on all his patients, a group that included some individuals who were sexual predators.

The idea of medically treating sex offenders, such as rapists and pedophiles, is not a new one. Both chemical and physical castration have been offered as "therapies" for sex offenders. Physical castration requires removal of the testes, which produce a major part of the male hormone testosterone that is responsible for sexual drive. Chemical castration uses drugs that block cells' reception of testosterone circulating in the blood and thus fools the body into reacting as though no testosterone were present. Although these treatments may reduce recidivism, they are barbaric because of their potential side effects, including feminization of the body and various medical problems. In contrast, treatment with SRI drugs involves medicines taken voluntarily by thousands of people for other psychiatric conditions, and the drugs have minimal side effects. Thus, SRIs could potentially treat large numbers of sex offenders, if controlled studies were to prove that the drugs were effective and safe for this application. As I write this chapter, the SRI drugs are not a proven treatment for sex offenders, but their existence as a medical treatment highlights the difference between a medical approach and a criminal justice approach to handling criminal offenders, a tension that is bound to become stronger as medical treatments for psychiatric disorders improve.

In this chapter, I first discuss the contrast between medical and criminal justice models of interventions for criminal offenders. Following this topic, I turn to other ethically sensitive areas at the juncture of biological theories of crime and social policy. My aim is not to resolve the policy and ethical issues presented in this chapter—a hubris that I do not possess—but, rather, to make the reader aware of these issues and to encourage genuine reflection upon them.

The Medical Model Versus the Criminal Justice Model

The criminal justice system operates under a particular concept of the criminal offender. I call this view "the criminal justice model." In this model, the criminal offender is basically an average Joe or Jane, a mentally normal and capable person. When confronted with the temptations of life, however, the individual makes a freely willed decision to violate the law for some gain. The offending act is intended; it is not an accident. For instance, skidding off a slippery road and hitting a bicyclist is a terrible accident. To hit the bicyclist while trying to scare him off the road is an intended criminal act, even if the outcome is worse than was anticipated. As a result of an offender's criminal act, he or she must be punished by the justice system. Punishment may involve a fine, imprisonment, or even the death penalty in a capital murder case. There is some proportionality between the crime and the punishment. It is proportionate to sentence a rapist to years in prison because of the psychological and physical harm a rape does to a woman. Giving an equal sentence to a boy who smashes a Halloween pumpkin would be regarded as ludicrous, a sentence vastly disproportionate to the offense.

In medieval times, before the state assumed the responsibility for imposing punishment, justice was often handled by the wronged family. Family members would seek a personal revenge. In some situations, a murderer could absolve himself of his crime by paying a fine to the family of his victim. Personal justice, however, can evolve into blood feuds between families that disrupt a society. In modern states, it is a crime for someone from a wronged family to seek revenge against the offender. The state's criminal justice system must impartially impose some sanction against the offender. In the United States, a trial by jury, with the presumption of innocence, is held to determine the defendant's innocence or guilt—did Joe or Jane commit a crime? After the jury renders a guilty verdict, a second court hearing may be used to determine the appropriate justice system punishment. In many states, federal sentencing guidelines that specify the length of prison sentence or the fine required for a particular criminal offense have reduced the "free hand" of a trial judge to impose any penalty.

The medical model contrasts sharply with the criminal justice one. According to the medical model, a criminal offender's behavior may be the result of a psychiatric disorder. The proper approach in this case is first to diagnose the disorder. Instead of a jury trial, an offender enters the health system to be diagnosed by a medical practitioner using a combination of a psychiatric interview with whatever specific psychological or medical tests are indicated. After diagnosis, a treatment plan is drawn up that might include medication as well as counseling sessions. Notice that the concept of the offender's criminal act is also different. Instead of exercising free will, the criminal is seen as acting on the basis of an underlying psychiatric disorder. Thus, a woman who compulsively shoplifts items of small value might be seen as having an obsessive-compulsive disorder. She would be prescribed an SRI medication as a treatment and monitored by her psychiatrist for treatment compliance and effectiveness. The criminal behavior is seen as just one more symptom of an underlying disorder.

Do criminal individuals have a psychiatric disorder? In some cases, they clearly do, yet offenders are still usually prosecuted under the criminal justice system because a plea of "innocent by reason of insanity" has become difficult to sustain. Russell Weston, Jr. killed two Washington, D.C. policemen near congressional offices and wounded a tourist (Clines 1998). A loner with a history of psychiatric hospitalization, Russell was wounded in the exchange of gunfire and was quickly caught. He was hospitalized for schizophrenia and cannot be tried until his sanity is restored by medical treatment. His lawyer opposed the medical treatment, because restoring Weston to sanity would make him face a possible death penalty if convicted for the double murder. Proper medical treatment might have avoided this tragedy. Yet do we force medical treatment on people who, possibly because of their mental illness, do not want it? Do we sentence someone to death who is insane?

Only a minority of criminals receive a diagnosis of a major psychosis, such as schizophrenia. However, the specter of medical treatments looms larger as we consider criminal dispositions such as those caused by attention deficit hyperactivity disorder (ADHD) or conduct disorder. Such disorders are common in the childhood backgrounds of adult criminals. Children possessing them often receive some kind of medical treatment, such as Ritalin (methylphenidate) for ADHD symptoms. Medications have been used for some time to treat childhood behaviors that in adolescence or adulthood are regarded as criminal. However, ADHD is no longer seen as just a childhood disorder, and Ritalin is now prescribed to adults for ADHD symptoms (Wender 1995).

Consider as an example an intervention to reduce symptoms in ADHD children, aged 6 to 13 (Barkley et al. 1989). The ADHD children were divided into two groups: those displaying aggression and those without aggression but with a greater level of inattentiveness. The subjects received a placebo (an inert substance), a low dose of

Ritalin, or a high dose of Ritalin. Both the children and investigators were unaware when a child was receiving the placebo or medication; that is, the study was "double-blinded." Both the aggressive and nonaggressive ADHD children improved while on medication, and many symptoms showed greater response at the high than at the low dosage. According to teacher ratings, the mean number of conduct problems decreased from 9.4 when aggressive children were on a placebo to 6.9 when on a low medication dose, to 5.8 when on a high medication dose. Parents also reported a decline in behavioral symptoms in response to medication. This intervention success does not mean that all children responded; the medication was more effective for some children than for others, and many children had to have their dosage readjusted after the study was completed. Furthermore, the treated aggressive children did not improve quite as much as the treated nonaggressive children. However, what this study demonstrates, as do many other studies like it, is that the kinds of behaviors that were once mainly in the province of the criminal justice system are now regarded as within the medical care system.

To think of these models in another way, under the medical model complete free will is not presumed. Instead, people are seen as inclined or predisposed by their biology toward criminal behavior. The markers of criminal disposition covered in previous chapters, from single genes to resting heart rate, are interpreted as showing a nonvoluntary greater chance of criminal behavior in those individuals possessing a criminal disposition than in those individuals without one. Now, it is probably an oversimplification to say that the criminal justice model assumes complete free will. Rather, it holds that it is best to treat people as possessing free will for their actions when deciding on how to respond to their criminal behavior. Thus, the criminal justice system can impose a severe penalty on an individual who has a low IQ, even though most people would not regard him as having the same judgmental capacities as an individual with a high IQ. The criminal justice system also weighs more than just an offender's guilt or innocence in its legal decisions. By punishing the offender, the justice system may satisfy the longing for revenge felt by many injured parties to a crime. In addition, punishment is seen as deterring people from committing crimes—we have all noticed how quickly traffic flow slows when a police car appears, as drivers quickly decide to obey the speed limit. Suddenly adopting a medical model in place of a criminal justice one might carry the risk of ignoring the accumulated wisdom of hundreds of years of English common law.

I should also mention that not all biological viewpoints insist on the abnormality, in a psychiatric sense, of individuals who might possess a criminal disposition. In particular, some evolutionary scholars would view many criminals as "normal" because they are merely pursuing an alternative behavioral strategy to obtain reproductive success (Mealey 1995; Rowe 1996). Under this theory, the "symptoms" of psychiatric genetics become healthy behavioral traits that optimize a particular outcome. A short attention span keeps one focused on the opportunities for sexual conquests and mating; aggression is used to deter rivals for mates and can be more effective than negotiation in the short term. The criminal may have a shorter life span than the conforming citizen, but a criminal may also have a greater number of biological offspring in that time span than a long-lived conformer. If the criminal disposition is, for the most part, a normal set of traits with a long evolutionary history, should drug treatments be forced upon the people who possess them? The criminal disposition may seem biologically nonadaptive because it inflicts pain and suffering on others more so than on its possessor. Yet many violent people report a greater self-esteem level than ordinary people do (Baumeister, Smart, and Boden, 1996). And, unlike people with other psychiatric disorders, they do not ordinarily volunteer for psychiatric treatment.

I have highlighted some of the points of tension between the medical and criminal justice models. Although the future is always difficult to predict, I anticipate that the legal system will move toward medical interventions for offenders. I have spoken to people in the juvenile court system in Chicago and already, informally, many juvenile delinquents receive psychiatric care and treatment. Thus, while the "medicalization" of the criminal justice system is unofficial, in some jurisdictions it is already taking place. Drug courts, which are widespread around the United States, may serve as a model for how medical treatments might be applied to adult criminals. In a drug court, offenders are required to not use illegal drugs and receive random urine or blood tests to confirm their abstinence. If they fail a drug test, they may be sent to jail to serve out the remainder of a prison sentence. A similar system could be imposed for sentences that rely on compliance to taking medications. The offender would be sentenced to receive psychiatric medication and counseling and would be released into society. He would then be periodically tested for compliance using blood or urine samples and would be watched to insure that no other conditions of his release were violated. If the tests indicate that the offender has not been taking the medication, he could be incarcerated to complete a prison sentence.

Biological information might also play a role as a mitigating factor in sentencing decisions. Because a biological predisposition implies less free will in committing a criminal act, a prison sentence could be reduced to reflect this impaired decision-making capacity. In the 1991 case of 25-year-old Stephen Mobley, his lawyers asked that genetic evidence be admitted to demonstrate his diminished capacity (Deno 1996). Mobley's crime was the cold-blooded killing of the manager of a Domino's Pizza. After robbing the store, he shot the manager in the back of the neck. One piece of evidence that Stephen's lawyers wanted to present was his family tree. Mobley's kin included several people with violent or criminal histories—for instance, Johnny, a cousin who was jailed off and on; Dean, a cousin who spent his adult life in prison for robbery and drug sales; and Bert, an aunt with a violent temper. In addition, his lawyers offered to have Mobley take biological tests for markers of criminal disposition. In the end, the court refused to consider any of the biological evidence, and Mobley's death sentence was not commuted.

In a less publicized case in Tucson, Arizona, however, a death sentence was commuted partly in response to genetic evidence. John Eastlack bludgeoned an elderly couple to death in their home. He was sentenced to death. An appeal of the death penalty, vigorously led by his adoptive mother, was based on the idea that John had a biological predisposition toward crime because, despite having been adopted into a middle-class family, he had exhibited severe behavior disorders from a young age. The original judge had retired from the case and a new judge heard this appeal; Eastlack's death sentence was reduced to life imprisonment. As this example shows, biological evidence may be slowly making its way into the courts as it attains a higher level of scientific acceptance.

Using Biological Markers to Predict Future Characteristics

Another ethical concern is the use of genetic tests to forecast future characteristics. An individual's genes are present in a fertilized egg cell that divides to become a whole human being. In the case of some fertility clinic procedures, a genetic forecast can be made *before* the implantation of an embryo. In in vitro fertilization, a sperm cell enters an egg cell in a lab dish and the resulting zygote commences its early cell divisions. A single cell, if taken from the newly dividing embryo, can be used to diagnose the embryo's genotype using molecular genetic tests. If the embryo contains an unwanted genotype, it may not be used and another embryo without the undesirable genotype can be implanted in the mother's uterus. This method of selecting for genetic characteristics is difficult and expensive, but couples have used it.

Predicting Adverse Medical Conditions From Genetic Information

Later in pregnancy, genetic tests may reveal a medical condition in a developing fetus, whether conceived naturally or via in vitro fertilization. These tests are usually done on fetal cells obtained by amniocentesis, in which amniotic fluid is withdrawn from around a fetus; other methods can also be used to obtain fetal cells during a pregnancy. After genotyping the fetal cells, a decision may be made to terminate a pregnancy on the basis of genetic markers. For example, many couples decide to terminate a pregnancy if a fetus tests positive for Down syndrome, which produces not only mental retardation but several medical complications (Plomin et al. 1997, 22–24). Down syndrome is not strictly a single-gene disorder; it is instead caused by an extra copy of chromosome 21. Currently, the practice of aborting Down syndrome embryos has resulted in reduced numbers of Down syndrome children born in states such as California.

In high-risk families, or in selected ethnic groups that carry a particular risk gene at a relatively high-risk frequency, there are also genetic tests available for many severe single-gene disorders. Tay-Sachs syndrome and sickle-cell anemia, for instance, are single-gene disorders that can be detected by genotyping fetal cells (Ridley 2000).

Genetic evidence for some diseases creates ethical dilemmas and hard personal decisions. Consider the BRAC2 gene that increases the risk of breast cancer in women. This gene acts in a genetically dominant fashion—a single copy of the gene increases the risk of breast and ovarian cancers. To illustrate this effect, by age 70 the risk of breast cancer in an average European women is about 5 percent. For women carrying one of several mutations in the BRAC2 gene, the risk is 33 to

46 percent (Thompson and Easton 2001). Thus, a woman carrying a mutated BRAC2 gene may have as much as a nine times greater risk of developing breast cancer by age 70 than an unaffected woman, and a 33 to 46 percent risk is substantial for such a fearsome disease.

Consequently, in a family with breast cancer cases, a cancer-free sister may decide to have herself genetically tested for BRAC2 genotypes. Upon learning of a positive finding, some women have had preventive surgery to remove their breasts—a drastic response for a statistical risk. Other women have decided to receive more frequent mammograms, used to detect breast cancer. Another ethical problem arises because once one family member has been tested, another who may have wanted to be uninformed about her cancer risk may learn that she has a 50 percent likelihood of carrying a mutated cancer gene. Should she get the same test, or avoid it? How are sisters' relationships affected by this genetic information? From these examples, you can see that genetic knowledge rests on the horns of serious ethical dilemmas.

Predicting Criminal Disposition From Genetic Information

At first glance, it might seem that genetic information could pose the same kinds of dilemmas for criminal disposition as it does for Down syndrome or breast cancer. However, this kind of knowledge is currently more in the realm of science fiction than science fact. A genetic diagnosis has a practical application when large, single-gene effects are found but not when genetic effects are weak. To return to Robert Plomin's catchy acronym, OGOD genes—one gene, one disorder—lend themselves to predictive genetic tests. Most people would base a decision about a serious medical condition on an increase in risk from 5 to 40 percent, but not from 1 to 1.7 percent.

For the genes involved in complex behavioral phenotypes, the effects of single genes will be much weaker. Suppose a gene were discovered that increased the risk of conduct disorder in childhood in males from 3 to 4.5 percent. That is a relative risk increase of just 1.5 percent. It is also a situation in which most gene carriers do not exhibit conduct disorder in childhood. On the basis of such weak evidence, I doubt that parents decide to abort a fetus or to go childless. And because conduct disorder may be mitigated by environmental influences and may be treatable, there are other reasons for hesitating to use genetic information alone.

With a larger number of genes, prediction of future conduct disorder might improve, but the difficulty of genetic engineering also increases. Instead of discarding just a few fetuses, parents might have to abort many to get one with a low genetic risk. And with the milder cases, there is not really much cause for concern—in the murderer Stephen Mobley's family pedigree, one brother channeled his aggression into becoming a self-made millionaire!

Although probably not useful for genetic testing, biological information about criminal disposition might, in time, be used along with knowledge about behavior to channel children into more appropriate treatments. Psychiatric diagnoses are currently based on questionnaires or interviews that count various behaviors and assess their severity. When John and Bill get into a fight on a school playground, their underlying neurology could be much different. Bill might have the low resting heart rate sign of biological risk of aggression. He might also have particular genes that increase the risk of aggression. Together with his observed fighting, the biological tests would confirm that he is a better candidate for a medical intervention than John, who may lack the biological indicators and who may have gotten into the fight in self-defense. Comings (personal communication) has suggested that biological tests might help identify individuals in a prison population who are the best candidates for a medical intervention. Although prisoners are savvy enough to lie on a pencil-and-paper test that could get them out of prison and into a treatment program, they cannot fake a brain scan of cerebral volume or a genetic test. Thus, combining the interview or questionnaire information with biological tests might give qualifying criminals an opportunity for medical treatment.

Another concern is the use of biological tests to mass-screen children for a criminal disposition. In this scenario, thousands of children would be genotyped, or given brain scans, and based on the results would be put into treatment programs, which might be required by a coercive law designed to reduce crime rates. This scenario seems far-fetched. For one, biological and genetic tests are costly; such a program would be expensive and therefore unattractive to politicians. A greater limitation, though, is that any mass screening program is likely to fill treatment centers with false positives. A false positive case occurs when someone who receives a positive test result is actually unaffected, as when a woman receives a false positive on a pregnancy test. Unless the biological tests were extremely sensitive, like a good pregnancy test, they would always generate many more false positive cases than truly affected cases, especially for disorders that are relatively uncommon. Overburdened treatment centers would find themselves treating many children who needed no treatment, and a public outcry would surely follow. Rather, I believe that children will continue to be referred to treatment programs first and foremost for their behavioral symptoms. However, genetic and biological tests may, in the future, help improve the treatments given to those children who are referred for help.

In the Name of Eugenics

Chapter 1 introduced Francis Galton as the founder of behavioral genetics. Galton (1869) also contributed a second, more controversial legacy: a goal of genetically improving the human race, for which he coined the name *eugenics* (meaning "wellborn"). Eugenics is a public policy of curbing the reproduction of less "fit" members of society and encouraging that of more "fit" members. In the case of Galton's nineteenth-century England, eugenics translated into encouraging the reproduction of middle- and upper-class English families, ones not dissimilar to Galton's own, and discouraging that of the economically disadvantaged. Eugenics became a broad social movement in England, in other European countries, and in the United States. Although the idea of eugenics is frequently thought of as a politically conservative one, it was a movement with broad support on the political left; Fabian socialists were among the early supporters of eugenics, while the Catholic church opposed it.

Eugenics and Public Policy

In England, the eugenics movement, while popular, had little influence on public policy. In the more pragmatic United States, a number of states passed compulsory sterilization laws that were enforced against individuals thought to have low IQs, particularly among the rural and urban poor. In a 1927 Supreme Court decision in *Buck vs. Bell,* the court upheld the right of states to sterilize mentally retarded persons (Degler 1991, 47–48). The decision concerned the constitutionality of a Virginia law that permitted the involuntary sterilization of persons in state institutions. In an oft-quoted statement in his legal opinion, presiding justice Oliver Wendell Holmes, Jr., wrote, "Three generations of imbeciles are enough." Since 1927, this Supreme Court decision has not been overturned.

Nonetheless, public opinion turned against the eugenics movement for many reasons (Degler 1991). One reason can be understood only in retrospect. Some people in the eugenics movement failed to understand the Mendelian mechanism of genetic inheritance; they thought it could be Lamarckian—that is, that characteristics acquired environmentally in the lifetime of the individual could be passed on to children genetically. When Lamarckian inheritance was conclusively disproved, a eugenics supporter could not be an environmental social reformer who advocated improving children's lot in life by environmentally helping their parents. Geneticists were discouraged from eugenics by the observation that, even if reproduction were restricted, generations would be needed to purge a population of an unwanted recessive gene.

Eugenics was falling out of favor with behavioral scientists long before the start of World War II. However, it was the atrocities of the Nazi regime against Jews, Gypsies, homosexuals, the physically handicapped, and other groups, justified in part by a theory of the biological superiority of a blue-eyed, blonde-haired Aryan race, that ended any appeal that eugenics may have had and nearly stopped post-1945 biological research on complex behaviors as well.

Social policies that broadly restrict human reproduction are bound to be unpopular, because most people want one or more children. And even if an individual does not desire a child, he or she probably still wants the opportunity to make the choice. Yet, to be effective in a genetic sense of changing a trait mean in a population, a eugenics policy would need to be broadly applied, and that broad application would undermine public support for it.

To limit its exploding population growth, China has adopted a one-child policy. This policy is more popular (from what I can tell by my limited contact with Chinese graduate students) in the Chinese cities, in which the crush of a large population is self-evident to all, than in rural areas, in which many people still want large families. This policy is not a eugenic one because it is (at least in theory) applied to everyone. Thus, the policy cannot decrease the frequency of some undesired genetic characteristic in the Chinese population. However, Chinese law does permit eugenic policies against persons thought to be mentally retarded or psychiatrically disturbed—laws that are strongly opposed by scientific societies for genetic research. There has not been pronounced opposition to these policies in China, but any opposition that exists might be hidden behind China's lack of political freedoms.

Before casting stones at the Chinese for their policies regarding reproduction, we should recognize that the federal government in the United States also develops public policies with the explicit or implicit intention of affecting reproductive rates. These policies are not eugenic as Galton defined it, because they lack the goal of genetically improving *Homo sapiens.* Nonetheless, they do aim to change the reproductive behavior of certain groups to reduce the burden of social problems on society. For instance, in the mid-1990s, the federal government permitted waivers of the welfare law so that states could experiment with different legal requirements. Many states adopted a family-cap provision such that welfare mothers were not to receive payments for each additional child born. Previously, more income was received for each child born to a welfare mother, a situation different from that for working mothers who would not automatically receive a pay raise for each child added to the family. The implicit message of this policy change was this: Welfare mothers should not use welfare payments to increase family size. Other policies have aimed at reducing the birthrates of unwed teenage mothers. These policies enjoy strong public support even though they attempt (not with terrific success) to manipulate the reproductive behavior of young women. For good reasons, the U.S. government avoids any truly eugenic social program. Nevertheless, if not always forthrightly stated, changing people's reproductive behavior has been a target of public policy in this country.

Eugenic Policies and Criminal Disposition

Some analysts fear that finding genes for a criminal disposition might reinvigorate some kind of eugenic action on the part of the U.S. government. I find this outcome unlikely. As a national policy, eugenics has been discredited, and it is unlikely to be embraced again. The genes that contribute to a criminal disposition are probably not infrequent in the population. For example, an allele of the DAT1 gene that contributes to attention deficit hyperactivity disorder is also the most common allele (Waldman et al. 1998). It would be impractical and difficult to try to rid the population of such common alleles, even if a eugenics program were created.

Although I do not think it is likely, a BRAC2-type gene might be discovered that has a major influence on the development of a criminal disposition, perhaps indirectly through producing a childhood behavior disorder. Such a gene might then be used in genetic counseling, and a fetus carrying the gene might be aborted on the basis of parental choices. This is a kind of eugenics, but it is one sharply different from Galton's original vision. Reproductive choice is made individually and independently by parents, who must weigh the decision to terminate a pregnancy against the seriousness of a behavioral disorder and their own values and ethics. Is such a policy eugenic? It would be so only if parents' individual decisions gradually lowered the gene frequency of the BRAC2-type gene. Such a change would occur slowly and would not be anything of concern for many years.

Despite the various fears surrounding the human genome project, my guess is that the prediction most likely to come to fruition (not immediately, but within 100 years) is the use of genome information to create handsomer men and more beautiful women, who are longer-lived, smarter, and healthier than today's average. In short, the road we may go down is not what people most fear in their children, but rather what they most desire in them.

Why the Criminal Justice System Is Not Scientifically Based

In Phoenix, Arizona, Sheriff Joe Arpaio has built a media-enhanced reputation with his public-appealing reforms of the criminal justice system. A weekly figure on local television news shows, Arpaio has built a tent city for felons, imprisoning them behind tall, wire fences. His tent city has a neon sign reading "vacancy"; Arpaio promises there is always room for one more prisoner. He dresses inmates in bright, pinstriped pajamas and makes their lives difficult in many ways. His tents lack air-conditioning, which in the Arizona summer is a hardship. Meals for the prisoners cost less than fast food: At an average cost of 45 cents per meal, the food is nutritious but not tasty. Arpaio pleases the public, but does he reduce the recidivism rate of the criminals, once they are released? There is no ongoing evaluation of his many "reforms."

In medicine until the early twentieth century, a visit to your local doctor was more likely to speed you to an early end than to cure you. Like Arpaio's reforms, various treatments were applied to patients with little idea of their true effectiveness. Some treatments were, in fact, highly ineffective, such as bleeding the patient. Other treatments were more effective, such as—although it sounds terrible—applying leeches to an infected wound. Medicine could only move beyond often inaccurate, and sometimes downright fatal, customs and conventional wisdom to consistently effective treatments by learning more about the underlying biology of disease and by adopting an experimental method to evaluate whether a medical treatment was truly effective.

In this regard, the criminal justice system is hampered. Our understanding of the causal basis of criminal activity has made progress, as shown by the biological studies of criminal disposition summarized in this book and by work on environmental influences as well. However, with a few exceptions, controlled experimentation is largely absent in the criminal justice system. Sheriff Arpaio believes that old-fashioned prison garb will help reduce recidivism, perhaps because it is so embarrassing. However, his idea could only be tested by randomly assigning some prisoners to wear it and others not to do so.

Although this example is offered with a bit of humor, the problem clearly exists for nearly all justice system reforms. The justice system has not, for both practical and ethical reasons, adopted an experimental approach using randomized treated and untreated groups. With any kind of experimentation with a criminal population, there is always the chance that one released prisoner in the experimental group will commit a terrible crime, resulting in a flurry of bad publicity and probably ending the treatment program. There is also the problem of obtaining consent from prisoners, who by their very situation are subject to coercion. Finally, sentences handed down by judges, and other legal barriers, also restrict the ability of the criminal justice system to experiment. Yet, without some kind of experimental work, we cannot accumulate good evidence on what works and what does not. Compared with medicine, the criminal justice system is more buffeted by the winds of public opinion, and reforms like Arpaios' that look backward instead of forward hardly demonstrate that the justice system is able to gain greater effectiveness.

Conclusion

This book has charted the general landscape of biology and crime. I have made the argument that biology causes a criminal disposition composed of personality traits and particular ways of thinking that increase the risk of criminal acts. I have emphasized the complexity of the criminal disposition on the biological side, as well as its interactions with the environment. The biological map extends from the most reductionistic—single genes related to criminal disposition—to the broad "why" questions of evolutionary psychology about what causes people to lie, cheat, and kill one another.

Several findings stand out. Behavioral genetics has contributed to the knowledge that many traits related to crime are heritable. Specific biological markers for a criminal disposition have been found, such as low resting heart rate and a reduced volume of the prefrontal cortex. The evolutionary approach gives an intellectually consistent explanation for a cross-cultural universal: the greater aggression of men than of women and the near absence of homicides in which one adult woman kills another. Variation in genes in the dopaminergic system are associated with attention deficit hyperactivity disorder in childhood. Mental illness involving the major psychoses explains many seemingly inexplicable killings. Aggression has been discovered to peak not at age 17, but in the toddler years; luckily, most babies cannot inflict severe harm on one another.

New discoveries will be made, some of which may change or qualify conclusions offered in this book. You are invited to participate in these disciplines examining the biological bases of criminal disposition—as a consumer, a user, or a beginning researcher. Learning a little biology does require stretching the mind, but it's always healthy to expand one's horizons with new intellectual and work challenges.

This book does not claim that biology is the only cause of crime; such a claim would be shortsighted. It claims only that we will learn more by looking at biological and environmental influences together and, for many students, this goal means learning more about the biological bases of behavior.

Recommended Reading

Degler, C. N. 1991. *In Search of Human Nature: The Decline and Revival of Darwinism in American Social Thought.* New York: Oxford

University Press. This book is a detailed history of ideas about biology and society from the 1800s to the 1990s. As with any detailed historical work, at times the arguments are complex and difficult, but the reader will be rewarded with a deeper understanding of the place of biology in social thought.

References

Barkley, R. A., M. B. McMurray, C. S. Edelbrock, and K. Robbins, K. 1989. "The Response of Aggressive and Nonaggressive ADHD Children to Two Doses of Methylphenidate." *Journal of the American Academy of Child and Adolescent Psychiatry* 28: 873–881.

Baumeister, R. F., L. Smart, and J. M. Boden. 1996. "Relation of Threatened Egotism to Violence and Aggression: The Dark Side of High Self-esteem." *Psychological Review* 103: 5–33.

Clines, F. X. 1998. "Capitol Hill Slayings: The Overview; Gunman Invades Capitol, Killing 2 Guards." *New York Times*, July 25: A1, A9.

Comings, D. 1998. Personal communication (November).

Degler C. N. 1991. *In Search of Human Nature: The Decline and Revival of Darwinism in American Social Thought.* New York: Oxford University Press.

Deno, D. W. 1996. "Legal Implications of Genetics and Crime Research." In G. R. Bock and J. A. Goode (eds.), *Genetics of Criminal and Antisocial Behavior*, pp. 248–256. Chichester, England: John Wiley & Sons.

Galton, F. 1869. *Hereditary Genius: An Inquiry Into Its Laws and Its Consequences.* London: Macmillan (Cleveland World Publishing Co., 1962).

Mealey, L. 1995. "The Sociobiology of Sociopathy: An Integrated Evolutionary Model." *Behavioral and Brain Sciences* 18: 523–599.

Plomin, R., J. C. DeFries, G. E. McClearn, and M. Rutter. 1997. *Behavioral Genetics*, (3rd ed.) New York: W. H. Freeman.

Ridley, M. 2000. *Genome: The Autobiography of a Species in 23 Chapters.* New York: HarperCollins.

Rowe, D. C. 1996. "An Adaptive Strategy Theory of Crime and Delinquency." In J. D. Hawkins (ed.), *Delinquency and Crime: Current Theories*, pp. 268–314. Cambridge, England: Cambridge University Press.

Slater, L. 2000. "How Do You Cure a Sex Addict?" *New York Times Magazine*, November 19, 96–102.

Thompson, D. and D. Easton. 2001. "Variation in Cancer Risks, by Mutation Position, in BRACA2 Mutation Carriers." *American Journal of Human Genetics* 68: 410–419.

Waldman, I. D., D. C. Rowe, A. Abramowitz, S. T. Kozel, J. H. Mohr, S. L. Sherman, H. H. Cleveland, M. L. Sanders, J. M. C. Gard, and C. Stever. 1998. "Association and Linkage of the Dopamine Transporter Gene (DAT1) and Attention Deficit Disorder in Children: Heterogeneity Due to Diagnostic Subtype and Severity." *American Journal of Human Genetics* 63: 1767–1776.

Wender, P. H. 1995. *Attention-deficit Hyperactivity Disorder in Adults.* New York: Oxford University Press. ✦

Author and Subject Indices

Author Index

A

B

C

D

E

F

G

H

I, J

K

L

T

U, V

W

X, Y, Z

Subject Index

A

B

C

D

E

F

G

N

O

P

Q, R

S

T

U

V

W

X, Y, Z